An Eastern Odyss
Adventures of Edward Enfield

Edward Enfield

Table of Contents

The Old and Infirm have at least this Privilege, that they can recall to their Minds those Scenes of Joy in which they once delighted, and ruminate over their past Pleasures, with a Satisfaction almost equal to the first Enjoyment. The Amusements of our Youth are the Boast and Comfort of our declining Years.

From the Preface to The Chase by William Somerville, (1675-1742) published 1735

Preface

This is mainly an account of my life in the East sixty years ago, when Hong Kong was a British Crown Colony, when the Japanese had little idea of how to make motor cars and Thailand was a country to which no-one went on holiday. Who am I, you may ask, to have the temerity to write what is undeniably autobiography? I can only say that having cycled in France and Greece, Ireland and Germany, and written books about that, I thought that something on the same lines about my Eastern adventures might be acceptable. There are not many of us left who have ridden as amateur jockeys in Hong Kong or been friends with the war-time commandant of the Bangkok prison camp. Those were interesting times, and they deserve to be recorded. To such reminiscences I have prefixed some glimpses of my earlier life as a schoolboy, as an undergraduate at an Oxford quite different from the Oxford of today, and as an inefficient officer in a cavalry regiment. I hope this might revive memories of past times in some, and perhaps cause an occasional smile to them and others.

Chapter 1

0-10

I was born on 3rd September 1929 in Hampstead, at 48 Downshire Hill, or possibly 44. I am not sure which, as I was very young at the time.

I have one sister called Clarissa who is nearly 6 years older than me. I could not say Clarissa and I called her Dissa, and this name has stuck to her so she is always called Dissa in the family. A man called Noel Iliffe, who was a BBC producer, once asked if it was short for Disappointment but this was just his joke. She was never a disappointment to me but I was rather a nuisance to her, as she was made to take me to Hampstead Heath and to the Round Pond to feed the ducks when she would rather have been playing with her friends.

Next door to us in Downshire Hill there was a lady called Mrs Carline and two girls called Unity and Shireen. Their name was not Carline but Spencer as they were the daughters of Stanley Spencer, the famous painter, and I think Mrs Carline was their grandmother. They were quite nice in spite of their strange names and used to come and play in our house, and I in theirs.

Unity, Shireen and I were all sent to the Montessori School in Hampstead where I pointed out to one of the teachers that a notice board had the word DOG spelt backwards. She asked me if I knew what it was spelt forwards and I said I didn't, but I did. I just thought God was someone you did not talk about. I did not learn much at the Montessori School. My mother once asked how I was getting on and they said "Edward is too busy showing off to the girls to have time for anything else." So then they sent me to the Hall School in Hampstead where there were no girls.

At the Hall School they had very nasty sausages for lunch on a certain day of the week which might have been Thursday. I remember this because there were a lot of Jewish boys who could not eat pork so there was macaroni cheese for them instead. Once I discovered this I used to become a sort of honorary Jew on Thursdays and go along with the Jewish boys for macaroni cheese instead of sausages.

I was not learning much at the Hall but my mother said she would give me two and sixpence if I was top of my form so I got to be top and got the money. Then they moved me up a form and I got to be top again, but when I was eight I was taken away and sent to boarding school, I don't know why. I rather liked the Hall and did not much like the boarding school, so it was a silly idea to send me there, but in those days this was what people did with boys, and some people still do. I did not get to be top of any forms at this new school but I remember getting 0 out of 100 in a geography exam. I could never do geography, which was a nuisance later in life when I was working for a shipping company as I found it hard to remember where the places were that the ships were going to.

The boarding school was called Abinger Hill. It was in Surrey and had big grounds with lots of rhododendrons, and I have disliked rhododendrons ever since. My locker number was 36 and locker number 35 belonged to a boy called Desmond Forbes-Adam who used to twist my arm. I did not like him either; in fact he was worse than the rhododendrons. But to be fair, Abinger Hill was alright as far as prep schools go. There was only one sadistic master and he was fired pretty quickly and the bullying was nothing much compared to what you read about at other schools. There was a boy called Jopson whose nickname was Jeep. Sometimes on a wet afternoon when there was nothing much to do a ring of boys would dance round Jopson in a circle and chant "penny a peep at the gandy Jeep" until he became furious. This was a rotten thing to do and boys can be rotten fellows when they feel like it.

My best achievement at Abinger Hill was to win the under ten 100 yards race. My aunt Nancy was supposed to come to take me out to lunch on sports day but she did not come till after lunch so I did not get any lunch. All the other boys had big picnics with their parents or a big lunch laid on by the school to impress the parents and this must have slowed them down, so I won. I got a small silver cup which is now lost. This was my only sporting achievement, as I was not much good at football and hopeless at cricket.

My father was not rich, but most of the boys at Abinger Hill had rich parents and many went to Eton, unless they were too stupid, in which case they went to Stowe. There was one who was a viscount. His father was the Marquis of Queensbury and he was the Viscount Drumlanrig. He was a nice chap, about the same age as me and he brought his own pony to the school and kept it at a riding school nearby. I have eaten many meals in the company of the Marquis of Queensbury, which he now is. I remember this but he would not as I have not seen him for 73 years and unfortunately I have not become famous and made a lord or anything like that.

We called the viscount "David Drum" and he became quite famous afterwards, not just for turning into the Marquis of Queensbury but also for being Professor of Ceramics at the Royal College of Art and for having a large number of children. Some other Abinger boys also became famous, such as Sir Edward Boyle who was Secretary of State for Education and Sir Peregrine Worsthorne who edited the Sunday Telegraph and is now well-known for his flowing locks and remarkable clothes, such as purple velvet plus fours.

At the start of one term a German lady called Mrs Schonfeld came to the school with her son who was around seven or younger. She did not speak much English and her son did not speak any at all, owing to their being German as I said before. They were German Jews who had got away from Hitler but had no money, so the headmaster of Abinger Hill School, Mr G. J. K. Harrison, took them in. He gave Mrs Schonfeld a job as a matron and her son came to the school, which was a good deed by Mr G. J. K. Harrison. Mrs Schonfeld had a hard time being a matron and not speaking good English but Schonners, as we called him, was alright. We felt sorry for him as he was small and did not speak English so we did not give him a hard time. Anyway he soon learned English and when he was grown up he changed his name to Andrew Shonfield and became a famous journalist which was a fine result of the good deed of Mr G. J. K. Harrison.

The house in which we lived at 44 or 48 Downshire Hill did not belong to us but was rented. The lease ran out so my father wrote to the landlord to ask if he could renew it and the answer from the landlord was as follows:

Dear Sir
I want nothing more to do with you.
Yours faithfully

This was a remarkable letter but even more remarkable was the envelope in which it came. In big letters on the back were the words BEWARE OF LAWYERS! Underneath in smaller print was a lot of stuff about how dishonest lawyers are and how it is best to have nothing at all to do with them. My father thought he had better look for somewhere else to live but one day the doorbell rang and on the doorstep was the landlord who said, "I have come to talk about renewing your lease".

"I thought you didn't want to" said my father.

"Oh yes I am sorry about that letter. It is just the thought of all those lawyers – 'my client this' 'your client that' – I cannot stand it!"

I don't know why but we did not stay in that house. My father could have bought it if he had wanted, and it would now be worth a huge amount of money, but he didn't, which is the kind of thing that is apt to happen. We moved to a maisonette at 12A Eton Road. We had the upper floors and down below was a man called Mr Courtney who did not like noise. If we made too much noise Mr Courtney used to go to his front door and slam it as loudly as he could. One day I accidentally rolled a cricket ball down the stairs, and every time it went Bump Mr Courtney went Slam. My father, who was generally a mild man, lost his temper, seized a mallet out of the tool chest and banged on the floor above Mr Courtney's head, but he had to stop as he sprained his wrist.

As well as renting a house in Downshire Hill, or a maisonette in Eton Road, my parents had a cottage in West Sussex which was very uncomfortable. It was in the middle of some woods, half a mile from the road down a very muddy lane and it had no electricity or main water. You had to pump the water out of a well and there was no bath and the lavatory was a nasty bucket which my father used to empty into a hole in the garden. When it got dark they lit candles or paraffin lamps and they had to cook on a paraffin stove. The cottage was too uncomfortable for us to go there in the winter but we went there for the Easter and summer holidays and I loved it.

About 200 yards away was another cottage where the Beesons lived. They lived there all the time because Mr Beeson was a groom and they were very poor and had nowhere else to live although their cottage was just as uncomfortable as ours. There were five children and one day when I was about four I went along and asked if I could play with them and they said I could. I learnt some new words when I was playing with them and I used these words when I went home and my mother got frightfully cross and sent me to bed. I did not know what these words meant and nobody told me what was wrong with them but I learnt that I must only use them when I was playing with the Beesons and not when I was at home. I may say that there were quite a lot of things that nobody explained to me, such as the riddle, "When is a door not a door?" I knew that the answer was, "When it's a jar" and I could see that if a door turned into a jam jar it would no longer be a door, but I had no idea why or how such a thing should happen. I did not raise any difficulties, I just accepted the whole thing as a mystery of life.

I liked the Beesons a lot. They could do clever things like making a trap out of bricks to catch birds, and they had a terrier which used to go into the brambles and catch a rabbit, which they took home to eat. This would have been useful as Mrs Beeson had to go out to work as a cleaner because Mr Beeson was not paid much as a groom which is why they did not have a lot of money for food or clothes, as you could tell by looking at them, because their clothes often had holes in them. They used to tell me about the village school where they said they got the stick if they did not behave well, and they were all very bright. Ollie became a Royal Marine and Norman went to South Africa and Giles became Head Lad at a racing stable and married a rich owner. Later on he became a racehorse trainer himself but I do not know how well he got on. The girls were called Sissy and Twinny and I do not know what happened to them but I expect they did alright as they were very bright as well.

When we were in our cottage my father spent most of his time mending the lane. He was always mending the lane as it was so muddy and about half a mile long. He got old bricks and stones and filled in the muddiest bits and sometimes he filled them in with logs. When the time came for my father to sell this cottage one of the people who came to see it was Randolph Churchill who got stuck in the mud and very cross, and swore a lot, but did not buy the cottage.

Although my father spent nearly all of his time mending the lane he did manage to find long enough to quarrel with one of the neighbours although it was not his fault. Two of our neighbours were identical twins, like Tweedle Dum and Tweedle Dee, and we could not tell them apart, which was awkward as my father only quarrelled with one of them. They both had farms and our cottage was in the middle. One day my nurse took me for a walk in the field opposite and the owner came and said, "What are you doing here?" My nurse said, "Mrs Enfield said it would be alright," and he said, "Mrs Enfield has the cheek of the devil," so then my father felt obliged to quarrel with him. He sent a letter demanding an apology and they did not speak for nearly 20 years. After that they made it up somehow and my parents were asked to a cocktail party where the quarrelsome twin was wearing white trousers which made it easy to tell him from his brother. My father was talking to Colonel Osmaston, a retired colonel of marines, who pointed across the lawn and said, "Who is that little counter-jumper I've just been talking to? Leconfield this – Cowdray that – who the devil is he anyway?"

"You mean the one in the white trousers?"

"Yes."

"That one is our host."

My mother was very keen on the Bloomsbury set and especially on Lytton Strachey although he was dead at the time of which I write. I think he must have been a stupid fellow as he proposed marriage to Virginia Woolf although he was the sort of man who does not like women of whatever sort at all, so that was a silly thing to do. Virginia Woolf drowned herself in a pond, which was another silly thing to do, but all the same my mother thought they were marvellous. Virginia Woolf did not think my mother or my father was marvellous. My mother's maiden name was Hussey, and V. Woolf wrote unpleasant things about her in her diaries, such as "Hussey has married the dullest man in England." I have not read V. Woolf's diaries or any of her novels as I wish to serve her right for being unpleasant about my parents. I just know about the unpleasant remarks in her diaries from looking up Enfield and Hussey in the index but I would not like to part with any money in her direction even though she is dead, so I do not buy the books.

Lytton Strachey had a sister called Marjorie who was a great friend of my mother and used to screech a lot. My mother said that all Stracheys screech but this is not true. There was another sister called Dorothy who married a French painter called Simon Bussy and she did not screech at all. On the other hand they had a daughter called Janie and she used to screech all right so the truth is that some Stracheys screech and some do not.

My mother thought that Marjorie Strachey was marvellous and my sister Dissa thought she was marvellous so I thought she was marvellous as well because I did not know that it was possible to think anything else, but now I am not so sure. She used to talk a lot of nonsense such as when she said that Lipizzaner horses were born white and turned black, which is just the wrong way round, and anyway she didn't know anything about horses so I don't know why she said it. But as she screeched so loudly it was not possible to argue with her, and as everyone thought she was marvellous, I suppose she was alright on the whole.

On my tenth birthday war was declared. We had no wireless set at our uncomfortable cottage so we walked half a mile down the lane to a neighbour's house where we listened to Mr Chamberlain telling us that we were now at war. My parents were a bit upset but it didn't matter to me and I had a jolly good birthday. Since then some kind person in government has said that anyone who was more than ten years old when the war started should be given a free passport for the rest of their lives. I think it is a reward for living through the war and perhaps helping to win it. The man from Sri Lanka who runs the local post office thinks it is very funny that I had to give him £80 for the passport which I would have got for nothing if I had come into the world a little sooner, but I have known better jokes.

The war did not make much difference to anything at first. There was bad news after a time but we never thought it possible that we might lose. Then in the summer of 1940 a rumour ran through the school, in the way that rumours sometimes did run through it, (such as that Monkey Sutherland had got a scholarship, which was true, or that Hobson had been expelled, which was not) that the school was going to Canada, and this was true. People thought the Germans were going to invade England and so someone arranged for our parents to send us to Canada if they wanted. Of about seventy boys at Abinger Hill School, something like fifty of us were sent off, with a few from other schools as well. Some sisters came, but not mine as she was 16 by then and people of that age were not allowed to leave but had to stay and help to fight the Germans.

We all thought that going to Canada was a great idea, except for a boy called Thomas who cried and said he thought he might never see his mother again. This was rather wet of him as the rest of us thought that stopping work in the middle of the summer term and getting on a boat to

Canada was a simply wizard notion. Then my mother came to say goodbye and gave me two Mars bars, which made things even better.

We went by train to Liverpool and got onto a boat called the Duchess of Richmond and sailed into the Irish Sea and were terribly sick. We were in the third class in the lower parts of the Duchess of Richmond where it smelt of oil. When the Duchess of Richmond went up we sank down in our bunks and when she went down we went shooting up and after a bit of that we were all sick. The only thing that cheered me up, and it did not cheer me up much, was thinking that if there were any rich people in the first class getting sick it did not matter how rich they were, there was nothing they could do about it as they could not get off.

I should say that Mr G. J. K. Harrison, the headmaster, came with us to see that we were alright, which was a big responsibility for him, as I came to see later. He made us wear lifejackets all the time in case the Duchess of Richmond was torpedoed by the Germans (which was a wise precaution as later on they did torpedo another ship and a lot of children were drowned. After that they did not send any more children to Canada).

I was sharing a cabin with the Viscount Drumlanrig who told me that he had been thinking hard about what he was really good at. He was alright at football and cricket, and he could ride pretty well, but he had decided that the thing he was really good at was paddling a canoe. We thought this would be pretty useful in Canada as we supposed that people travelled by canoe quite a lot, unless they lived in the parts where people travelled on horses.

We went up the St Lawrence River and got off the Duchess of Richmond at Montreal and went by train to Ottawa, after which life took a different turn altogether.

Chapter 2

10-14

We were quartered on a school called Ashbury College, and I have since been told that when we arrived it was on the verge of bankruptcy. I find this easy to believe, partly because it was such a rotten school, but mainly because it was half empty and so had room to take in about sixty boys as permanent boarders. It is now a most thriving establishment, and I know this because they send me their annual magazine although I have pleaded with them not to, and to save the postage. Perhaps it is rather unkind of me, but I really have little interest in knowing that people of whom I have never heard are getting on very well at whatever it is they happen to be doing, which is the sort of thing that fill the pages of the magazine. Even the obituaries are a disappointment as they do not seem to pick up the deaths of old Abinger boys but just report upon dead Canadians. Nevertheless, as they are so kind as to send it, I know that Ashbury is now in a fine state, its survival at a critical time having been due to us.

Partly this was a matter of money, as the Abinger parents went on paying the Abinger fees which were somehow transmitted to the Ashbury bank account. Then the status of the school was much improved by this influx of boys who in many cases were potential Etonians and had among them an undeniable viscount. It became the thing for the children of ambassadors to be sent to Ashbury, and so the social tone went up and it became, in time, very prosperous.

There are several mysteries around that time. I have said that a number of sisters came with us, and I can think of six. I have no recollection of seeing them on the Duchess of Richmond, so perhaps they had better cabins than the steerage accommodation where we boys were. We arrived at Ashbury in the middle of the summer holidays when the buildings were empty. I know that the girls were with us for a time but then they disappeared, and I have little idea of where they went, or how they managed. I met some of them back in England after the war, and they made passing references to happy times, but where they lived, how they were taught, what happened in the holidays – I never asked and so these things are all unknown. I know, though, that Mrs Jo Harrison, the headmaster's wife, was with us and that she took charge of the girls, while he was responsible for the boys.

In many ways he had responsibility without power, because we were largely at the mercy of Ashbury. Mr Jim Harrison, as I came to know him, had no way of seeing that we were well taught, and we were not. He could not take any of us away if we were suffering, and some were. He himself taught at the school, so I suppose he had a salary, but I believe that money was always tight. When it came to the school holidays the whole responsibility was his, and he managed somehow, but it must have been hard. Nevertheless when, after the war, some of us met again at Abinger reunions, nobody seemed to bear a grudge, but then, of course not everyone came.

One of Mr Jim Harrison's difficulties must have taken the form of a pale and podgy man called A. D. Brain. The titular headmaster was called Archdale, and Mr Archdale had a beard, which gave him a Grecian look, and had been a soccer blue at Cambridge. I believe he must have got the job on the strength of his beard and his blue, because he seemed to have little influence upon what happened, except that he coached the Ashbury soccer teams which always won, rather than the Canadian Football teams, which were coached by A. D. Brain, and always lost. The school was really run by A. D. Brain, who was the deputy head and a great believer in fear as an instrument of discipline. He used to beat boys pretty regularly and I was told that he hated Jews and beat Jewish boys with a special ferocity. I do not remember any Jewish boys coming to the Abinger reunions and they may well have had painful memories of Ashbury and kept away.

I am glad to say that I was never beaten by A. D. Brain, but I had an immediate taste of his style. On the day after we arrived we were all ordered into the gym, where we lined the walls while A. D. Brain paced up and down, telling us what a marvellous school we had come to, and how lucky we were to be there. Suddenly he said, "Did you put your tongue out at me?" – a question which nobody answered as nobody had put their tongue out, thought it wasn't a bad idea, at that.

"You!" he said fiercely and I realised he was glaring at me.

18

"No sir," I said. "I didn't put my tongue out."

He marched across, seized me by the ear, and banged my head against a vaulting horse. "Stay there till I tell you." So I stood with my back to the proceedings while he went on about the great merits of this bleak and mediocre school.

I do not say that this was a very important episode. I was not scarred for life, but it is an indication of the sort of regime run by A. D. Brain. I think he may have been slightly mad. I say this because we later found that about twice a term he used to disappear completely for two or three days, and neither he nor anyone else ever said anything about it. He might have had a migraine, or a hangover, or a fit of depression, all of which is mere speculation as he simply vanished. No attempt was made to replace him, and the boys in his classroom posted a look-out in case he turned up and ragged around and chatted. If he went missing on Tuesday he would come striding into class on Thursday or Friday and carry on exactly as if he had been there all week. If not mad, it was certainly eccentric.

Our first summer holidays went on in a fairly bleak way. There was a lake near the school where we could bathe, but the mosquitoes found our fresh English blood to be so delicious that I was covered with bites and looked as if I had chicken pox. A friendly man took a party of us out to a country club and gave us Coca Cola and ice creams, which was kind of him, and then a marvellous thing happened. I was sent for by Mr Harrison, and in his study found a very nice looking lady who said she was Mrs Lambe. Mr and Mrs Lambe wanted to know if I would like to stay with them for a couple of days, and I said I would, because I definitely liked the look of Mrs Lambe, in which I was right.

She took me to their country cottage across the river from Ottawa in Quebec province, beside the Gatineau River at a place called Kirk's Ferry. There was Mr Lambe, who said I should call him Uncle Morris and Mrs Lambe, who said I should call her Aunt Helen and their son Ron, who was two years older than me and went to Ashbury. There was Uncle Morris's sister whom I called Aunt Margaret and her daughters, Peggy and Caroline, who were perhaps five and two years older than me. There were some cousins and other young people living around, so there was a good deal of bustle and activity and they were all very friendly and kind. The house had something in common with my parents' Sussex cottage, except that it was made of wood and there was no well. The drinking water came from a spring which bubbled up some way off and Ron and I used to fetch it in buckets. We bathed in the Gatineau River, and water for washing was river water. The lavatory was a horrid little shed in the woods in which I felt quite at home as it was like the one in Sussex.

The entertainments were firstly swimming in the Gatineau and I couldn't swim, but they set about teaching me, and I pretty soon got the hang of the breast stroke which is the only stroke I have ever mastered. Huge quantities of logs used to come floating down the river, encircled by a boom of what looked like railway sleepers chained together, and one of our sports was to go out with an older boy by motor boat and walk round on the top of the boom. If anyone had slipped and fallen inside among the logs I should think the chances of being drowned would have been pretty high, but nobody slipped, nobody drowned, and nobody worried.

A single track railway ran beside the river, and in the early mornings the driver used to hoot as the train passed by, so then Peggy and Caroline waved at him without getting out of bed. We used to walk along this track to the nearest store where we bought Pepsi Colas or ice creams. Thinking of this track reminds me of Natalie, although it all happened, so far as it happened at all, three years later.

Natalie was a friend of Caroline's who came to stay at Kirk's Ferry. She was dark, very pretty indeed, also very kind, and she was the first person with whom I fell seriously and hopelessly in love. It was hopeless because there was an impassable barrier between us, as she was then 15 and I was only 13. This didn't stop me falling in love, but there was nothing to be done about it. Natalie understood my difficulties exactly, and was extremely nice to me, which possibly made it worse. One day we were walking along the railway track, I along the sleepers and she balancing on one of the rails as if it were a sort of tightrope. She put her hand on my shoulder to balance herself, which was a thrill in itself and I would have liked to have walked on like that forever. Then she said, "It's a pity you're not two years older or you could have been my feller." The thought of being Natalie's feller was so utterly blissful that it made me completely speechless, and then she was sorry because she thought she had embarrassed me, which indeed she had. Like the Marquis of

Queensbury, Natalie will have forgotten me by now, but I have not forgotten her as you can see, and I do hope that life has been kind to her as she was so very nice to me.

The one aspect of Kirk's Ferry that I did not like was the gramophone. A lot of teenagers used to gather at the Lambe's cottage in the evenings and dance to terrible records. I shudder even now as I think of the Chattanooga Choo Choo, which was going to choo choo me home, or so the record said. Then there was the idiotic one which went "A tisket, a tasket, my little yellow basket." There was a peculiar record which went as far as I remember:

"Hut sut, ralston on the rirrela-ra
With a brawler brawler soo-eee".

I never saw the words written down but that is what they sounded like and I think that they were meant to be Swedish or something. There were others equally awful but the selection was small and so everything was played over and over again. It was alright for the teenagers shuffling about in the gloaming while clasped in each other's arms, but I had no part in that, I just had to bear the music which I could not escape. Three years later the records were still the same but there was the added suffering of seeing Natalie clasped in the arms of Tommy Green.

After two or three days of my first visit Mrs Lambe, otherwise my Aunt Helen, said to me, "How would you like to stay with us for good?"

"Stay with you instead of at Ashbury?"

"Yes, live with us but still go to Ashbury."

"Oh yes please".

So I did. I became a day boy at Ashbury and lived with the Lambes for the next three and a half years. I am amazed at the kindness of my Aunt Helen and Uncle Morris. They treated me exactly as a son. They fed me, clothed me, gave me pocket money, bought me a bicycle, took me on holiday, gave me such things as skates and skis and football boots. My Aunt Helen was very beautiful and my Uncle Morris was quite a wag, and they were both extremely kind so I was very happy. I do not know why they adopted me like this. They were not enormously rich. No other Abinger boy was taken into a family. Perhaps they thought that England was bound to lose the war and that I would be theirs forever. Ron was their only son, and no doubt they thought that I would be company for him, but I am very sorry to say that this did not work. He did his best to look after me at first, but somehow we had nothing in common, so after a time I made fresh friends and he went off with his, and we kept to ourselves.

I have said that my Uncle Morris was quite a wag, but perhaps the Canadians have a style of humour of their own. The Lambes had a dog, an English setter called Duke, and when Uncle Morris came back from work on a hot summer's day he always had the following conversation with Duke:

"Hey, Duke – are you a hot dog?

Are you ever a hot dog, hey Duke?

Yes sir, I can see, you certainly are a hot dog.

My word yes, you are a hot dog, hey Duke?"

I think there were more permutations as it seemed to go on for a long time. Duke enjoyed the attention and used to wag his tail, and we all treated it as a fresh and original joke, although it happened every day throughout the summer.

When I went back to Ashbury at the beginning of term I found that I had been put in a higher form than Ron Lambe, which was awkward, and may have given the impression that I was frightfully clever, which was not the case. It was possibly to do with the state of Canadian education in general, or perhaps of Ashbury in particular. Mr Jim Harrison must have taken a look at the sort of thing that was being taught in different forms, and allocated us accordingly. He may not have realised that, while Abinger Hill was certainly no forcing house, we were about three years ahead of the Ashbury boys so that I, at the age of 11, was in a form of English boys of 11 or 12 and Canadian boys of 14 or 15. It stayed like that all the time I was there. Ron Lambe very sensibly objected to this and had himself transferred to another school called Lisgar. This cannot possibly have done him any harm as he could not have been worse taught at Lisgar than we were at Ashbury, at least in the lower forms.

Perhaps the pay was very bad, because an equal collection of deadbeat teachers would be hard to find. There was one master who more than once came into class drunk, put his feet on his desk, went to sleep and snored. There were others who could not keep order, and we ragged them furiously. A boy called Dan Farson, later to become some sort of TV celebrity, was a master of teacher-baiting. His technique was to suck up to any new teacher when he or she arrived, so that they thought that in him they had a friend, and then to turn and rend them when they least expected it. I recall his doing this to an unfortunate French woman who tried to teach us French and made the mistake of saying "Fingers!" instead of "Hands up!" Instantly Dan Farson was waving his fingers in the air and shouting, "Fingers, fingers," and then we all were waving our hands about and shouting "fingers" making life impossible for the poor lady, who never knew where she had gone wrong.

Perhaps the saddest of all was a man called Mr Kay who looked like a character called Keyhole Kate in either the Dandy or the Beano comic, so he was nicknamed Keyhole Kay. We used to bait him by putting the tip of the right thumb and forefinger together and peering at each other through the hole so made. To be fair there were exceptions. A clergyman called Dr Boone arrived to teach us maths as well as scripture. He wore buttoned up boots which could only have been fastened with a button hook, and we took this as a sure sign that we could rag him, but we were wrong. He quelled an incipient riot in an instant, tore us off a communal strip, and after that taught us algebra and geometry without any difficulty.

When I was 13, I arrived in the top form where we were taught Ancient History, French, and Latin by A. D. Brain. He carried a lot of ancient history in his head and used to pace up and down the classroom dictating facts about Egyptians and Hittites and Greeks and Romans, and we wrote these down in our notebooks. I would say this did me neither good nor harm. Latin he taught possibly well enough, except that he started at the beginning, as if we knew none at all, which may have been true of the Canadians of 17 or 18 but was not true of us Abinger boys who started Latin at the age of 8. French he taught well, and we read some advanced texts, including *Le Livre de Mon Ami of Anatole France* and the play *Andromaque of Racine*. Mr Harrison made a kind attempt to teach me a little Greek from time to time but I did not advance, so all in all, at the end of three and a half years at Ashbury, I had made progress in French and maths, and at the age of 14 knew about the same amount of Latin and rather less Greek than I had at the age of 10.

I liked Ottawa, but for a capital city it was not strong on amusements. There being no theatre or concert hall, the nearest approach to intellectual entertainment came in the form of ice hockey, all-in wrestling and two cinemas. I went to the cinema every Saturday, regardless of what was on, and with a Canadian friend I used to cheer for the Ottawa Senators on the ice hockey rink and to shout and yell at the heroes and villains in the wrestling ring. I was for a time quite friendly with an Ashbury boy who was later to achieve distinction. His name was John Taylor and he came close to becoming Prime Minister of Canada but he had an incurable habit of patting ladies on the bottom which led to his undoing.

*

In England, the threat of German invasion passed away, and gradually the seas became safer, so after about three years it became possible for us to go home. We did not go in a group but one at a time. There was still some risk, and the travel arrangements had to be kept secret so boys just turned up in England and telephoned their parents to say, "I'm back." I think some general inkling had been given beforehand – at least that is what happened to me. My father, who was a civil servant, came out to America for a conference and then came up to Ottawa. He stayed with the Lambes for a few days and in the course of his visit set me the most difficult diplomatic problem of my entire life. We were all together in their sitting room when he said to me, "I've been making arrangements to get you home." What was I to say to that? I could hardly say to my Aunt Helen and Uncle Morris, who had been so kind to me for all this time, "Oh good, I'm going to leave you." Neither was there any point in saying, "Oh dear, I would much rather stay here" although this was indeed the truth, as I was perfectly happy where I was and didn't want to go back in the least. As far as I remember, as I couldn't say either, "Oh, good," or "Oh, dear," I simply said, "Oh" and left it at that.

My father went away, time went on and an order came that I was to go by train to New York, take a taxi to the hotel Something and join a group for England. Uncle Morris and Aunt Helen saw me off from Ottawa station and my mother later took exception to a letter from Aunt Helen in which it said I looked forlorn. She read into it the implication that I didn't want to leave, which was certainly the case, but I thought I had kept it successfully to myself. When I got to the hotel Something in New York nobody knew anything about me and there was no sign of any group forming up for England. This was a bit alarming as I had very little money and no idea what to do if someone had blundered but there was nothing to do but wait. I went out into the street, but New York looked to be a dangerous place so I went back in again. Eventually some other boys arrived until there was a party of about twenty and then they took us to New York harbour and put us on an aircraft carrier. It was not an active aircraft carrier, as there were no planes landing or taking off and I think it was carrying cargo of some sort. I suppose we slept in the quarters where the airmen would have been if there were any. The two impressions that I have of life in the Royal Navy is that you sleep in bunks in which it is just as easy to be as sick as it was in the Duchess of Richmond, and that they wake you up in the morning by shouting obscenities at you from a loudspeaker, unless I misheard what was said. And so I got back to England, and somehow got to London, and telephoned my father in his office and said, "I'm back."

Chapter 3

14-18

The things that my mother found most objectionable in me on my return were that I wore a green suit, that I had a lock of hair like Hitler's which I used to push aside with my thumb, but which always fell forward again; that I had a Canadian accent, and that if someone said, "Thank you" to me I used to reply, "S'orl right, I'd do the same for a dawg."

I remember that green suit as I was proud of it. It was the first suit I ever owned, and it fitted me very well. I remember my Aunt Helen buying it for me, and that it was reduced in price, possibly because it was green and perhaps because it was double-breasted. I am not at all sure why it was thought to be so awful in England, but it may come as a shock if the first time you see your son after three and a half years you find him wearing a double-breasted green Canadian suit. Anyway, even in those days of wartime clothes rationing it was thought to be impossible that I should wear it, and after the day on which I arrived in it, I never saw it again.

Although it did not bother me, my Hitler lock was a continual problem to my mother, until it was finally solved about three years later when I was sent to have my hair cut by Trumpers of Curzon Street. Mr Trumper cut the king's hair and had the royal warrant, and he, or one of his staff, was a match for my troublesome forelock. The Canadian accent lasted about a fortnight as I was almost immediately sent off to board at Westminster School where I pretty soon took care to talk like everyone else. I was pained that, when thanked, my reply that I would do as much for a dog was not received as a bit of witty repartee. It was always treated as such in Canada, but having found that it failed in England, I dropped it from my repertoire.

Having been one of the younger members of the top form at Ashbury I now became the oldest member of the bottom form at Westminster, which was called the Transitus. This was galling, but they had overestimated my ignorance, and after a couple of weeks I was advanced to the Fifth form where I was about the same age as most people, and where I more or less held my own. Westminster was divided between King's Scholars and Townboys. There were forty scholars who were either King's Scholars or Queen's Scholars according to the sex of the sovereign at the time, and they were a sort of elite, having superior ideas from being on the foundation of Westminster Abbey and wearing gowns, and they all lived together in what was called College. The rest of us, called Town Boys, were an inferior breed scattered about in different houses, and were largely cannon fodder for the King's Scholars, who had the best of everything and were best at most things. They were top of all the forms, and won all the musical competitions and got the best parts in school plays and always provided the captain of the school, and their parents paid little or no fees however rich they were. There were a couple of King's Scholars in the Fifth form but most of them were too clever for that and started straight away in the Shell, which was the form in which the School Certificate was taken.

Westminster was divided in another sense because half of it was in Herefordshire and half in Worcestershire. In times of peace the school was in Little Deans Yard, next to the cloisters of Westminster Abbey, but it had moved to the country to escape the blitz. The King's Scholars, and my house which was called Rigauds, were in the tiny Worcestershire village of Whitbourne, while the other houses were near the Herefordshire town of Bromyard. We were five miles apart, so three times a week, wet or fine, we of the Worcestershire contingent cycled to Bromyard for lessons, and three times a week they of the Herefordshire party cycled to Whitbourne. The King's Scholars were, of course, housed in the best accommodation, in the form of a fine house with spacious grounds called Whitbourne Court, while we Rigaudites were crammed into the Whitbourne rectory in a suitably subordinate position.

My housemaster was a benign and elderly man who taught physics and had the nickname of Beaker. He was the only man I have ever known who wore spats, which was an odd thing for him to do in rural Worcestershire. He did not do it every day, but sometimes he would appear dressed in a black coat, striped trousers, black shoes and spats, which I suppose was the correct dress for a Westminster master before the war. On other days it would come home to him that he was in the midst of fields and orchards, and then he would dress as a country gentleman, sometimes going so far as to appear in breeches, boots and a bright yellow turtle-necked pullover.

The living arrangements were fairly rough. There was an old cow-house which had two baths, a cold tap and a copper. We junior boys had to take it in turns to fill the copper with cold water and then light and feed a fire under it. There was a rota by which everyone had a bath twice a week, by bailing hot water out of the copper with a long-handled bailer and topping it up from the cold tap. In another old cow-house were the lavatories, being four buckets side by side, each separated from the next by sackcloth curtains but open at the front, which I always felt to be the sort of thing one might find in a prisoner of war camp.

All the same, life was quite pleasant. Conditions were cramped and the noise considerable, but the regime was civilised. A neighbouring farmer had given us a field for football and cricket, and we swam in the river Teme in summer. The wartime food was better than I expected, as in Canada the British were thought to be on the edge of starvation. There was a revolting dish called Woolton Pie, consisting of root vegetables baked in pastry and served cold, but it only came up once a week. There were no fresh eggs, but the house won an inter-house football cup and somehow by way of celebration we each miraculously, and perhaps illegally, were given a poached egg for supper, which was the only egg I have ever eaten in the county of Worcestershire.

I had arrived in February. I left in July to spend the summer holidays in the uncomfortable cottage, which had now come up in the world. Builders had been called in, it was twice its original size and the plumbing arrangements were much improved. A telephone had been installed, but it did not have a dial, so you had to pick up the phone and wait till the village postmaster came on the line at the other end before you could make a call. He was a melancholy man, not over keen on his work, and if you made a call in the evening the first thing you always seemed to hear was a deep sigh, followed by Mr James' voice saying gloomily, "Somebody keep my dinner warm".

Towards the end of those holidays I went into a public ward in St Thomas's Hospital and didn't come back to Westminster until the following April. It was all to do with the way they used to grow corn. There were no selective weed killers so the cornfields were always full of thistles. There were no combine harvesters, so the corn was got in by hand. As the young men had gone to the war, the work was done by old men and young boys and, I suppose, by land girls, but there weren't any land girls on the farm near us. I was pressed into service and got a poisoned finger from a thistle in the corn, which somehow turned into something called osteomyelitis. This is Greek for inflammation of the marrow of the bone, and if you can imagine a terrible toothache in your left shin and right ankle, you will have a good idea of what it was like. As the young doctors had gone to the war to look after the soldiers I got into the hands of an old dodderer who had been fetched out of retirement and who didn't know it was osteomyelitis but thought it was rheumatism. The great danger of rheumatism, he said, was that it might affect my heart, and to avoid this I must lie still and could not possibly have any aspirin, which I suppose was the only painkiller available at the time. For two weeks I lay in bed without moving, in increasing pain, unable to get out of bed, beginning to rave and finally achieving a temperature of 104 degrees, at which point the old dodderer decided that perhaps it would be best if I went to hospital.

Part of St Thomas's Hospital had been evacuated from London to some Nissen huts near Godalming, and they took me there. It was glorious. A plump and friendly nurse gave me a bath so calmly and efficiently that I felt better at once. Then a doctor came along and prodded my leg, at which I said, "Ow."

"Sorry," he said, "but that is not rheumatism. I will send someone else." Then a one-legged surgeon came clanking along on his artificial limb and he too prodded my leg. "Ow," I said again.

"Sorry, but I know what that it is. That is how I lost my leg." Then he added as an afterthought, "Not that I'm going to let that happen to you." He inspired such confidence that I did not think for a moment that I might lose a leg and was perfectly calm when they wheeled me off to the operating theatre. There they gave me an injection in my arm and I just had time to say, "It smells of fish," before I passed out. I woke to find myself in bed in the middle of a long ward, with both my legs in plaster.

I can tell you, as a survivor of the hospital service before it got absorbed into the National Health Service, that it was superb. They were all so efficient. My bed was opposite the table where the Ward Sister sat, and each morning the night nurses lined up before her to render their reports, and were dismissed. Immediately after that the day nurses marched in, heads high, arms swinging, cuffs starched, caps properly adjusted, and fell in for inspection. When the doctors came on their rounds we had to tidy our lockers and lie straight in our beds. I never met anything like it till I did my National Service and arrived at Catterick Camp as a Royal Armoured Corps recruit. People say that the answer to the problems of the hospital service today is to bring back Matron, but I believe in Ward Sister. Matron in my day was a shadowy, distant figure who was talked about but seemed not to appear. I had imagined an imposing, Olympian figure, or perhaps a sort of female R.S.M., but when she turned up she proved to be a sweet little lady in a cloak who asked me in the kindest way if I was feeling better. I noticed though that the Ward Sister, though herself built in the Junoesque style, seemed to be considerably in awe of her, but all the same it was the Ward Sister who maintained discipline and ran the show.

Great harm was done to the NHS by the Women's Lib movement, as it opened up all sorts of careers to women and so created a shortage of nurses. In the time of which I write, nice girls commonly did a three-year stint of nursing, in transit, as it were, on the way to becoming wives and mothers, so I was nursed entirely by young ladies. They were all very friendly and some were very pretty, so I kept falling in love but they kept getting posted to other wards, so I was left desolate till I fell in love with a new one. My leg used to hurt at night, when they would give me a huge pill called Veganin which stopped the pain and sent me to sleep, but I always woke up in the middle of the night wet with sweat. Then two lovely night nurses, one fair and one dark, gave me a bath and dry sheets and fresh pyjamas with much whispering and giggling which disturbed the whole ward. I loved it, and them, but suddenly they disappeared, never to be seen again. St Thomas's was, as it still is, a teaching hospital and among other things the nurses had to learn to give injections, which many of them learnt on me. A wonderful new and very expensive drug had been discovered, called penicillin, which came in a thick and oily form to be injected through a big needle at the end of a small garden syringe. They injected it into me once every four hours for two weeks, and as it was a pretty simple thing to do, new nurses who had never done such a thing before were allowed to start by sticking this great needle into me.

There were medical students coming and going all the time, too much in awe of the Ward Sister to flirt with the nurses, but often stopping to chat to me. They were very keen on rugby football, at which there was keen rivalry with other hospitals, and there was always a sprinkling of black eyes and occasionally a leg in plaster. Once or twice I was lectured on. A student would be detailed off to mug up my case, and later he had to explain what was wrong with me to a group of his contemporaries plus a great man from Harley Street who had come down for the occasion and who tried to trip him up with questions that he hadn't thought of. It was a sort of fairly harmless blood sport which I rather enjoyed.

I should think there were about twenty four beds in the ward, ten down each side and four across the end. On my right was an old retired male nurse who had prostate cancer and on my left was a boy of about my own age called Arfer, who had an in-grown toenail. The nurses and doctors called Arfer "Arthur" and me "Edward" but everyone else was just known by their surname, such as Smith or Robinson, as if it was a prison. Arfer came from New Cross and was a supporter of Millwall, and he and I were two of the few who came there to get better, as most people died. St Thomas's must have had a special link to the police, as many of them were policemen and they seemed to arrive in a reasonable state but get weaker and weaker till one day screens were put round their bed and the next morning they were gone. I remember one stout-looking copper whom Arfer told me in awed tones had a beat in Whitechapel and was frightfully tough. At first he used to stride around the ward in a garish dressing gown but he had a brain tumour and lost all his hair from radiotherapy, and eventually died. This was nothing to do with the standards of care but I think it was mainly a cancer ward, and whether they operated or whether they tried radiotherapy, cancer nearly always won. It wasn't too bad a place to die, except at Christmas. They looked after us with endless patience and gave all the latest drugs and painkillers, but at Christmas it became quite festive and rather noisy, with medical students dressed as Father Christmas roller skating up and down the ward, all of which was hard on the relatives at the bedside of someone who was at death's door.

I did not get out of bed for three months, as my legs were in plaster for that time, but pretty soon I could sit up and read and write like anyone else. It was September, and in June I was to sit the very important School

31

Certificate exam, so I did a correspondence course in English and French, Latin and Greek, maths and history organised by Westminster School. They told me what to read and posted me exercises to do, and I did them and posted them back, and they marked them and sent me some more. In spite of the distractions of nurses, doctors, medical students, policemen dying and Arfer trying to get up pillow fights, it worked remarkably well. They sent me home after four months, and for the next two months I carried on with the correspondence course and then I went back to school. The result of my missing two complete terms was that I rose five places in the form order, and from having been fifth in the Fifth form I now came top of the Shell. This caused chagrin and annoyance to those King's Scholars who regarded this position as theirs of right, though to be fair I was at least a year older than the oldest of them. Also it taught me that schoolmasters don't matter all that much. You can manage very well without them.

During my first Easter holidays the Sussex woods had been crowded with American soldiers waiting to invade France. In the following term we huddled round the wireless to hear the reports of the D-Day landings. When I came back to Westminster next year we gathered round the wireless again, to hear the announcement of VE Day. At the start of the following term the school went back to London.

*

After School Certificate we had to specialise and I went in for Latin and Greek, which was called "going on the classical side" and was an act of some temerity. By custom and tradition the study of Latin and Greek at this level was the preserve of King's Scholars who had been crammed full of Latin and Greek at their preparatory schools, and in my remaining three years at Westminster, one in the classical Sixth and two in the Seventh, I was the only Town Boy in either form. The classical Sixth was taught mostly by the Master of the King's Scholars, a man with the nickname of Poon, and I always felt that Poon resented my existence. He did not like having a Town Boy in his form, and probably thought I was pretty stupid as I was a year older than all the clever young devils in their scholar's gowns. He certainly gave me no encouragement and liked to indulge his taste for sarcasm at my expense, but I didn't care much, owing to my discovery that schoolmasters are people you can manage without.

Two men did encourage me. The first was my housemaster who looked at my School Certificate results and said, "On the strength of this, I shall expect you to get election," which was Westminster coded language for getting a university scholarship. Nobody had ever said anything so encouraging before and it cheered me up no end. I was also encouraged by the very tall headmaster, J.T. Christie, nicknamed Legs, who was a fine scholar and had been an Oxford don as well as a schoolmaster. He had a huge enthusiasm not just for Latin and Greek but for all literature, and he did a very good imitation of Fagin in the condemned cell by wrapping himself up in his gown and curling up in the corner so that he looked just like Cruikshank's illustration in Oliver Twist. Legs seemed positively to welcome this errant Town Boy among the scholars, and at the end of my first term in the classical Sixth he wrote in my report, "He has certainly chosen the right subject for himself," which was one in the eye for Poon.

There was a good deal to be said for Westminster in those days. Their idea of specialisation was that we should do Latin, Greek, Ancient History and English, plus German, Biology and Art on the side. We learnt German in case any of us turned into serious scholars, in which case we would need to study the works of the eminent German classicists. We had lessons in biology because it was thought we should not go out into the word in complete ignorance of all aspects of science, and I don't really know why we had art lessons, except perhaps that there was an art master who had to be kept employed. I got nowhere with art, and have a mere smattering of German but can come out strong on the subject of Mendel and the sweet peas. I have heard it said that if a blue-eyed wife with a blue-eyed husband gives birth to a brown-eyed child it is a sure sign of adultery and grounds for divorce. This is not so, and if I met anyone who was troubled by this thought I could put their minds at rest by explaining about dominant and recessive genes, thanks to Mendel and the sweet peas.

Beyond that, there were thriving societies, in particular the debating society, which was guided by a small New Zealander called Wynstan Monk who could walk on his hands. He was actually the history master, but as there was no PE master he taught gym as well, which is why he could walk on his hands. He was a brilliant history teacher who got Oxford and Cambridge scholarships for boys who scarcely deserved them, and in terms of practical use in daily life what I learnt under his guidance in the debating society has proved to be of more direct use than anything else I can think of.

Westminster was also a rowing school, which was a great advantage. More or less anyone can row, and for me who has no eye for a ball it was exhilarating to find that I actually got into the second eight and rowed respectably against other schools. For any parent with a son who is mediocre at football and a duffer at cricket I would say, "Send him to a rowing school if you possibly can."

Among my contemporaries I hardly noticed a small, insignificant boy in another house until he became a large, significant man in the House of Commons, where he was Chancellor of the Exchequer. Later he went on a diet and is not as large now as he was before, but he remains significant as Lord Lawson of Blaby, leading the sceptical heretics who say the climate isn't changing against the orthodox vested interests who say it is. To which I say that Galileo was alone when he said the earth went round the sun, and he was right, so I hope Lord Lawson is as well.

I recall a boy arriving who said his name was Charles Crispin Cervantes Tickell, which naturally we supposed to be pronounced Tickle, but he said we were to say it "Tick-ell". Westminster was a tolerant school, so nobody punched his head or pulled his hair for having such a silly name, as a result of which he neither developed a stammer nor became a delinquent but went into the Foreign Office and became an ambassador. Years later he turned up in Chichester as a Festivity. That is to say, there were some goings-on which they called the Chichester Festivities and one of them was a talk on The Earth by C.C.C. Tickell, now known as Sir Crispin Tickell GCMG KCVO and I don't know what else besides. Being curious to see how he had turned out, I went, and he said there were four aspects to atomic energy, "like the Four Horsemen of the Apocalypse". I went home and turned up the Four Horsemen in the Book of Revelation and I couldn't for the life of me see any likeness between them and the peaceful uses of atomic energy, so I suppose that superior Civil Servants are programmed to talk like that. If anyone says anything about four anythings, they say "like the Four Horsemen of the Apocalypse."

*

34

While I was at Westminster my father rose through the ranks of the civil service to the point where he achieved the dignity of knighthood, and I got the morning off school to go to Buckingham Palace for the ceremony. Laurence Olivier was in the same group, but differed from the others because they had never been knighted before, whereas he had, often - indeed perhaps twice a day on matinee days. He therefore knew how to do the thing properly. We sat and watched while a man from the Ministry of Pensions shuffled forward, ducked his head in the way he had been told, and was tapped on the shoulder by the king, to be followed by an Air Marshall for the same treatment. When it came to Sir Laurence's turn his name was called but nothing happened, until we all looked round to see what was up, and then, and not before, he swept down the aisle and flung himself upon one knee before his sovereign, with a grand theatrical gesture as if he was being dubbed knight on the field at Agincourt. The king looked as if he thought it pretty odd, and seemed almost on the point of giggling, as well he might because Sir Laurence had bleached his hair and had a peculiar haircut, which I suppose was meant to make him look Danish, for purposes of filming Hamlet.

My father's knighthood had a greater effect upon my mother than on him. It coincided with her sudden conversion to radical socialism which she practised in Wisborough Green, in the heart of Sussex, and also in the constituency with the largest Tory majority in the country. She joined the Wisborough Green Labour Party, whose members were very glad to have her now she was a Lady. This may seem strange but the sitting MP was Lord Winterton, who was an earl. He was an Irish earl, and they are allowed to sit in the House of Commons, to which he was elected when an undergraduate at Oxford, and where he stayed until he became Father of the House. The Wisborough Green socialists talked incessantly about The Noble Earl and his Lordship's support for this and that, such as his presumed support for what they called the "iniquitous game laws" such being the burning topics of the day in Wisborough Green, or at least among the half dozen or so socialists to be found there. When my mother joined them they were very pleased because they felt that in Her Ladyship they now had a court card of their own, which they could play right back at His Lordship, though of course they had a false estimation of the value of the wife of a knight bachelor as against an Irish peer.

I once accompanied my mother and some of the brotherhood to one of Lord Winterton's meetings during an election campaign. The high spot of the evening was when His Lordship gave a neat answer to a hostile political question. I do not remember the question, but I shall never forget the answer, which was: "Take your hands out of your pockets when you speak to me." It was an answer which, had I been a floating voter, would have made me a lifelong Tory.

Before her conversion to Socialism my mother's main interest was in English Literature, which she always pronounced with a capital L. She now combined English Literature and Socialism. The entire membership of the Wisborough Green Labour Party would fit into the dining room of our house (which was known as "Her Ladyship's country residence") without the need for extra chairs, and they took to doing so. She formed them into a discussion group which, drawing on *Gray's Elegy*, she christened, "the Village Hampdens." The literary reference was lost upon them, but they took the idea on trust, and said how much they appreciated the revival of the fine old English custom of "having a hampden" and would frequently assemble to oppose with dauntless breast His Lordship and the iniquitous game laws. I told my mother she had struck a rich vein with the Hampdens, and it could be further developed with a poetry society called the "Mute Miltons" the Home Guard re-named the "Guiltless Cromwells" and a choral society called the "Noiseless Tenors".

*

At the end of my time at Westminster I managed to do what my housemaster Beaker had suggested and got a scholarship to Oxford, partly because classics was the easiest subject in which to achieve such a thing. The subject itself was not easy, indeed Greek and Latin are difficult languages, but the competition was less. There were as many scholarships in history as in classics, but far more people went in for history so you had to be cleverer to get a history scholarship than a classical one. Also, Westminster had a strong classical tradition. We were pretty well taught, the King's Scholars set a good pace, so I only had to keep my place in the middle of the pack to get to the right standard. The half-dozen of us who left in my last year all got scholarships or exhibitions to Oxford or Cambridge, and so it was that in October 1948 I arrived at University College, Oxford, as a classical scholar.

Chapter 4

19-22

Anyone who said that the late 1940s and early 1950s were a grim period in England is talking utter nonsense, and you can tell them so from me. Those who say such a thing are those who were not there, while we who were present and alive to what was going on know that it was a fine time.

"There was rationing," they say, and so there was, but it didn't matter as we were used to it. The nation was better fed than ever before or than it is now, as people did not starve, nor did they die from being too fat. Also, there was a certain skill involved in shopping, and occasional little triumphs to be won. Meat was rationed, but sausages were not, and whether or not you got any sausages was at the whim of the butcher. My mother once went to buy the meat ration and said to the butcher by way of conversation, "We are not having very good weather".

"Madam," says he, "we must take the weather that God sends to us."

"Yes indeed, but His ways are not always our ways."

"Madam that is very true and I can let you have a pound of sausages."

Nowadays you can buy all the meat and all the sausages you want without any skill at repartee, and shopping has been, as they say, de-skilled.

It was, say those who were not there, a time of austerity, and this is true, but we understood when Stafford Cripps told us we must Export or Die. All the nation's money had been spent on winning the war, and we accepted that it would take some time to get things straight. Above all it was a time of hope. The war was over, Hitler and Hirohito had been dealt with, and now things were going to get better.

*

The Oxford to which I went was recognisably the Oxford of my father's time and even of my grandfather's time, but when I go to Oxford now I see that the buildings are generally the same, but this is true of little else. We may not have been much to look at but we did not wear the frightfully scruffy clothes they go in for now, nor did we have Mohican haircuts or rings in our noses. The standard dress was grey flannels, sports jacket and tie, to which you added a gown if going to a lecture, tutorial or dinner. There were some who always wore suits; my friend George Byam-Shaw wore a bow tie, and occasionally Kenneth Tynan was to be seen on the High Street in a purple suit and white gloves, holding a silver-headed walking stick and looking like a resuscitated corpse. It was a strange thing about Kenneth Tynan that he always looked dead although, at that time, he wasn't.

We were not at uni, we were up at Oxford; we were not students, we were undergraduates, and here a great change has taken place. There are now three times as many people at University College, commonly called Univ, as there were in my time, and four out of ten are graduates. When I went up, post-graduates were about one in a hundred and the college was small enough for everyone to know everyone else. To make the college bigger they keep pestering us for money saying to themselves, "We *will* expand the college and the old members *shall* pay for it." I strongly suspect that if they had left things exactly as they were, teaching the same subjects and not adding bizarre new fellowships, they could have lived upon their income from their endowments plus moderate undergraduate fees and Univ would have been the most sought-after college at Oxford. Now they are much the same as anyone else.

They have admitted women. There used to be men's colleges and women's colleges, but now the sexes are all jumbled up, and I must say I don't like the sound of it. Univ recently sent me a glossy publication called The Martlet, named after the heraldic bird that appears on the college crest. This Martlet is a new venture, edited by a young man called the Communications Officer, a post unknown in my day and presumably paid for from the funds extracted from old members. It marks, he says, "A dramatic change in Univ's communications with its wider community", and it includes a contribution from the current President of the Junior Common Room. As this is an office which I held myself in my final year, I was interested to see what my successor had to say. "The welfare team" says she, for it is a woman, "have also organised for (sic) an expansion in the contraceptive methods available in college. Oxfordshire" (she means Oxford) "Council are (sic) one of the few city councils to provide the morning-after pill free of charge to students, and through discussions with college it has been made possible also to make this available and free to Univ students." We of the wider community may make of that what we will, but it seems to suggest that the female element is wildly promiscuous and not very good at written English and that the sort of thing that would have got us instantly sent down is now an everyday occurrence.

I feel sorry for them, that is the truth of it, because, say what you like, it isn't as good as it was. They live in nothing like the style that we did. When I went up to sit the Univ scholarship exam, I called on a friend who had been a year ahead of me at school and was now established at Christ Church. He entertained me in his rooms in front of a blazing open coal fire. College servants were known as "scouts" and one of the duties of the scout on his staircase was to climb the stairs each morning, take the empty coal scuttle down to the cellar, fill it up, carry it up the stairs, clean the grate and lay the fire. All my friend had to do was put a match to it, and the whole arrangement was perfectly reasonable as there was no other form of heating in his rooms. For two years I had a large sitting room and a small bedroom in college, and all of us on this staircase were looked after by a scout called Lesley. Lesley used to wake us each morning with hot water so that we could wash and shave. He cleaned our rooms, polished our shoes, made our beds, and did any washing up, which he really hated. There was never anything more than glasses or cups to be washed, but if Lesley arrived in the early morning to find such things he used to bang and clatter and swear loudly to himself. I lay in bed listening to Lesley going "Bloody Naafi do!" while he bashed the crockery about, before he came into my bedroom and politely poured the hot water into the basin on the washstand.

The scouts also waited in Hall, where we dined every night. We drank either beer or water, and if you wanted beer you caught the eye of a scout who brought it in a solid silver tankard. Each tankard had a date on it, and they were said to go back to the time of Charles II, as all the earlier ones had been melted down and the silver given to his father. Certainly there was a long continuous run of tankards, because every year those who were leaving would club together and buy another one. Now the young ladies and gentleman rarely dine in Hall, and there are no scouts so there is no use for the tankards, and I think they have lost the lot. I have twice asked what happened to them but nobody knew, and my wife tried to buy the one to which I had subscribed, hoping to give it to me as an 80th birthday present, but they did not answer her letter. One day perhaps someone will open a cupboard and find a horde of silver tankards of great value which they won't know what to do with.

We scholars had to take it in turns to say grace in Hall. Univ has a long Latin grace of three sets of responses, and two prayers, and the Master, or whoever was at the head of High Table, had it written on a card but we had to learn it by heart. The scholar started, *"Benedictus sit Deus in donis suis"* and the Master replied, *"Et sanctus in omnibus operibus suis"* and so it went on. If you could gabble through it at racing pace a huge cheer went up, but this was a risky business as if you stumbled you were sconced.

The sconce was a handsome silver tankard which I expect they have lost along with the others. It held two and a half pints of beer and was the regular instrument for maintaining discipline in Hall. If you were late, improperly dressed, swore, used foul language or erred in some other way, the President of the Junior Common Room or other qualified officer could be asked to sconce you. If he upheld the charge, which he always did, the sconce, full to the brim, was put before you by the butler. You could, if you wished, take a drink and send it on round the table, in which case you had to pay for the two and a half pints of beer. You had the choice, however, of trying to drink the whole lot in twenty five seconds, and if you succeeded, then whoever sconced you had to pay. At least, he had to pay unless he could drink another sconce in twenty five seconds, in which case you, the offender, had to pay for both.

Frank, the butler, would pull his stopwatch out of his waistcoat pocket and set it going as you started to drink. He was the arbiter as to whether or not you had "sunk" it within the time, and I couldn't do it, but there were those who could. One night Alan Stewart sconced Nick Gent, who sank it, so Alan Stewart called for a second sconce, and sank that. Nick Gent then called for a third sconce, and sank it. Alan Stewart called for a fourth sconce, and sank that one. Nick Gent then called for a fifth sconce, but Frank, the butler, stepped in and stopped it.

Hall was always full and the High Table well attended, as the dons of those days were proper dons. The college was their life, and those who got a fellowship tended to stay till they retired or died, whereas nowadays they are mostly passing through on something called a career path. The old dons came to Hall in gowns and suits, or sometimes dinner jackets, but now they go home to bath the baby and if they come to Hall at all they are as likely to wear jeans and a bomber jacket as anything else. I know this, because I have been back and seen it happening.

They used to have a leisurely dinner at High Table, and Hall was usually empty of undergraduates by the time they finished, but sometimes there would be a group still sitting and chatting when the dons rose. The Master would then read a short grace, and turn to the undergraduates and bow, and they bowed back. One night H. O. McWilliam, for whatever reason but perhaps being slightly drunk, forgot to stop and carried on with his bow till his forehead hit the table. This became an instant tradition, and from then on we always bowed like that, banging the table with our heads. The Dean rather disapproved of the habit of cheering when grace was said at top speed, but the sight of a group of undergraduates seeming to perform a sort of oriental kow-tow to the Master always made him laugh.

The Dean was Giles Allington. His great friend was Freddie Wells, the classics tutor, who asked him to be godfather to his son. Giles told me that he proposed to give the boy a silver christening mug with on it half a line of Homer, καί ποτέ τις εἴποι which means, "Then some man may say ..." leaving Freddie to supply the rest of the line, "πατρός γ᾽ ὅδε πολλὸν ἀμείνων" which means, "he is a much better man than his father". This was the sort of donnish tease they liked to go in for, and a more waspish version came down from the Ancient History tutor, George Stevenson, who was always known as Steve. His great delight was to bait the Master in the days when Sir William Beveridge of the Beveridge Report held that office, and once their conversation went like this:

Steve: You were at Balliol, were you, Master?

Beveridge: Yes, I was at Balliol.

Steve: Were there many *clever* men at Balliol, when you were there, Master?

Beveridge: Yes, there was a very clever lot when I was there."

Steve: Did you *know* the clever men Master?

I went up straight from school, but in 1948 there were still a good many undergraduates who had been in the war and had fairly recently been de-mobbed. The university had not yet thought of making changes to the pre-war regime, and one of the rules that survived was that we might not go into a public house. Now you can, if you wish, tell a man who has come through the Normandy campaign or flown dangerous missions over the jungles of Burma that he can't have a pint in a pub if he wants, but it doesn't work, as they don't take any notice. When some former flight lieutenant was quietly sipping a pint of bitter in the company of an ex-brigade major, in would come the Proctors' "bulldogs", these being college servants temporarily deployed to act as amateur policemen on behalf of the university.

"Are you a member of this university, sir?"
"Yes I am."
"Which college, sir?"
"Trinity."
"Your name, sir?"
"Brown".
"You've been progged, sir," and then Mr Brown would be called before the proctors and fined, I think, three pounds. It did not last though, and very soon the rule had to be abolished as being unenforceable.

*

Perhaps for the convenience of the college porter, or for our health, or for whatever reason, we were required to be back in college by midnight. If you banged on the gate after that the porter opened it and let you in, but also reported you to the Dean, who fined you a couple of pounds, so we didn't trouble the porter but climbed into college instead. I only did this two or three times but on the last occasion I found that the Dean had mounted an anti-climbing in campaign and barred the window I had used before. I knew of another route, which was to walk along the top of the wall of the master's garden, step onto the roof of a shed at the end and jump down. Once I was up on the wall I found the Dean had been there before me and there were coils of barbed wire all along the top, rather like those at the battle of the Somme. I managed to wade through these, came to a shed, stepped onto it and it collapsed with an enormous crash of corrugated iron.

I was not hurt, but next morning the Master, the Reverend J. K. Wilde, sent a note to Luther Vye, the President of the J. C. R. complaining that someone climbing into college had utterly destroyed his hen house. I asked Luther to write back and say that he had discovered the culprit, who was anxious to pay for the damage. Back came a reply from Master Wilde saying that, "the damage has proved to be easily reparable so no question of payment arises, and I hope that the gentleman concerned suffered no injury to his person in what must have been at the time an unnerving experience."

This idea of climbing into college was not something thought up by the heroes of Normandy or Burma but was a long-standing tradition throughout the university, as I learnt from a chance encounter in the high street with Mr J. T. Christie, my former headmaster. He had recently become Principal of Jesus, a college which then was full of serious Welshmen. "Enfield," he said, "Jesus is a strange college. When the old members of other colleges get together they say, 'do you remember when Charlie Adams was climbing into college and got stuck on top of the railings?' Not at Jesus they don't. At Jesus they say 'do you remember Professor Robertson's lectures? He was *magnificent.*'"

Having rowed at school, I rowed at Univ, and was in the first eight in three of the four summers I was up. Men were smaller in those days, and although I weighed little more than 9 stone I was still acceptable at the sharp ends of the boat, at stroke, at bow or at two. If I go to a wedding nowadays I see a succession of giants coming into the church, and I think what fine oarsmen they would make and how hopeless I would be in competition with them. We did reasonably well, all the same, and I have a fine photograph of the Univ eight about to bump St John's exactly opposite the Univ barge, myself at stroke and coxed by Peter Mumford, the future Bishop of Taunton.

I did not row in my last year as I thought I had better try to concentrate on my studies, which brings me to the serious side of life. The classics degree was a four-year course, divided into two, called Mods and Greats. For Mods they set you three years' work and gave you five terms to do it in, at the end of which there were twelve compulsory and two optional papers. Mods was to do with Greek and Latin language and literature, and Greats with Greek and Roman history, plus philosophy - Greek, general and modern. There were no 2-1s or 2-2s in those days, but in each part there were honours to be got. Most people got a first or a second; some got a third, and it was just possible to get a fourth but this was to live dangerously, as a fourth was too close to outright failure to be comfortable.

The complexities of all this are probably of little interest except to those who have themselves studied the classics, but for the benefit of any who are curious to know how it was done then, and perhaps to compare it with the way it is done now, I have sketched out the syllabus in an appendix. I got a first in Mods and a second in Greats, which is a sign that schoolboy learning and reasonable diligence could carry you through Mods, but Greats was more difficult and required intelligence. I have known men who say things like, "I missed my first" or "my tutor thought I would get a first" but this is humbug. Trying to pass yourself off as cleverer than you are is not only undignified, it doesn't work. If you got a second, a second is what you got, and no one will believe that it is some kind of a first in disguise.

My second in Greats was a safe second, neither a near-third nor a failed-first. I know this because of my viva. In Greats, but not in Mods, as the last step you had to appear in a dark suit, white tie, gown and mortar board before three of the examiners. If, on the strength of your written papers, you were on the edge of a class, perhaps either a very good second or a possible first, they asked you all sorts of questions to give you a chance to talk your way up, but if the outcome was clear anyway, the viva was a mere formality. You could never tell till you got there, so you arrived in a state of considerable anxiety. My viva was perfunctory, as was the viva of the man ahead of me, but for a very different reason. Whoever he was, as he sat down the chief examiner rose to his feet, removed his mortar board, and said, "Mr Robinson, my colleagues and I have read your papers with the greatest possible pleasure and instruction. Thank you very much." I have often wondered what became of this brilliant man, whose name was not actually Robinson, and I only called him that as I have forgotten his real name. Not surprisingly, he was a bit shaken, having braced himself for a possible grilling, and perhaps he would have liked a chance to display his brilliance under fire, but anyway he went away looking not so much delighted as positively stunned. As for me, they asked me a simple question about the Peloponnesian War, to which I gave a simple answer, and was dismissed.

The viva took place during the vacation, after we had all gone down, and then I was summoned to present myself at Catterick Camp in Yorkshire, on the 3rd September 1952, my 23rd birthday, to begin two years of National Service.

Chapter 5

Army

As a preliminary to Catterick I had been given a medical test and because of my earlier osteomyelitis my legs were declared to be B2, or something like that, which meant, they said, that I wouldn't do for the infantry. That didn't matter, as I wanted to do my service in a cavalry regiment in Germany because I knew that as well as tanks or armoured cars, they would have horses, and I was keen on horses at the time. Accordingly I opted into the Royal Armoured Corps, was sent to Catterick, and spent much of my two months there doing strenuous infantry training in the form of square-bashing, assault courses, route marches and other activities for which I was supposedly unfit.

As soon as we arrived they issued us with a lot of kit, injected us with sub-lethal doses of typhoid, cholera and lockjaw, and ordered us to sit on our beds and polish our boots and our brasses, and not to stop till they told us. When we began to recover our health they started us on foot drill, and from then on we divided most of our time between foot drill and polishing. We polished and wore our second-best boots, and we polished our best boots but never wore them. For two months nobody spoke a civil word to us except the Naafi girls and some ladies from the Blood Transfusion Service who came to take a pint from each of us.

Catterick camp was a bleak place, and we lived in wooden huts. They paid us 28 shillings a week and deducted 2 shillings and sixpence for barrack damages, although we never damaged the barracks. I can remember three others from our hut, all of us with the rank of trooper, which is what they call privates in the Armoured Corps. One was a public schoolboy called Jeremy Toop who became known as Jeremy Toop the Super Trooper. Then there were two Scots, one of whom was called Alec Alan. He was a farm boy who had never been away from home before, except to stay in something called a bothy and look after sheep. He called us all "friend" and used to make wise remarks on the lines of "a mon's best friend is his mither." He was very devout, and I think he found the constant blasphemy and obscenity of a barrack room to be distressing. The other Scot was a tough Glaswegian who, unlike Alec, had indeed been away from home before, having spent time in borstal. He said little and disliked noise, which I was glad about because barrack rooms can be noisy places, but if he said "be quiet" or some Glaswegian equivalent, nobody argued and everyone was quiet.

*

While I was at Catterick Field Marshall Sir William Slim KCB, GCMG, DSO, MC addressed a remark to me and 1,499 other people which I have remembered ever since. They told us that the CIGS was coming to see us. They did not tell us what a CIGS was, or whether it was a group or a person, but the news sent a shiver of excitement through the whole camp of, I guess, about 1500 men, and six Naafi girls. It also caused them to step up the foot drill and the polishing.

We learned that when the CIGS comes to see you the thing to do is march around in circles. A box was put on the barrack square on which the CIGS would stand, and for hour upon hour we practised marching in circles in front of it. Then we went back to barracks and polished some more.

When the day came we got up early so as not to be late, and actually put our best boots on our feet instead of on top of our lockers. It was the first of about six occasions in two years on which these boots were worn. We fell in at nine o'clock and marched to the barrack square, which took about ten minutes. Then we waited. Punctually at 11 o'clock a helicopter arrived and a CIGS got out, who I later learnt was Bill Slim. He got on the box and, as arranged, we marched around in circles. Then he made a speech.

The opening words of this speech comprised the memorable statement of which I have spoken. "The infantry," he said, "is the backbone of the army." This theme he went on to develop, and it may not seem at all remarkable until I explain that Catterick Camp was entirely given over to the Royal Armoured Corps and the Royal Corps of Signals, and of the 1,500 of us on parade, barring a drill sergeant or two, there was not a single infantryman present.

But we did not hiss or boo this man who had just told us we were of no account. We did not even throw down our caps and waist belts and declare, "We'll soldier no more, you may do what you please," as in the example given in the manual of military law. On the contrary, on the command, "Remove headdress" we removed our headdress, and on the command, "Hip hip" we raised the headdress to the full extent of the right arm, shouted "Hooray!" counted a pause of 2-3, and returned the headdress to the region of the left breast. We did this three times. Then the CIGS remounted his helicopter and flew away, and we marched back to barracks to repair the damage to our best boots.

*

It is said that Dr Spooner, after whom the Spoonerism is named, went to preach at Winchester College and by mistake took a sermon intended for a country parish, instead of the one he meant for the school. As a result he astonished the boys by telling them that, "All of your hands are horny with toil, and some of you are mothers." I suspect the CIGS did something similar.

After a time some of us, including the Super Trooper, were declared to be Potential Officers and put into a separate hut under the charge of a particularly ferocious sergeant. The chief effect of being a PO was that, instead of learning to be drivers, gunners or wireless operators like everyone else, we did more exacting foot drill and a higher standard of polishing was required. The good thing was that we did a 3-day course in driving and maintenance during which we did no driving and maintained nothing, as the whole thing was conducted in a classroom. We never got our hands on a lorry, let alone a tank, but all the same it was one of the most useful of the many courses I have attended over a long life. Up to that time I had not had the slightest idea of how the internal combustion engine worked, but now I learnt that it is based on something called the Otto Cycle, which goes Suck, Squeeze, Bang, Blow. Suck was petrol gas being sucked into a cylinder; Squeeze was the gas being squeezed by a piston going up; Bang was the gas exploding and driving the piston down, and Blow was the exhaust fumes being blown out through a valve. They explained that the constant repetition of this astonishing process in several cylinders one after the other made a motor car go along. To make the gas explode, a spark was required, and this was provided by a spark plug. And so on. It was a revelation, and although there was no practical content to the course, I could see what was wanted and was enabled later in life to change the oil of a car or clean the plug of a lawnmower, and furthermore to understand why I was doing it. Not only that, but the knowledge I picked up has allowed me to play a part in conversations from which I would otherwise have been excluded. I have no interest in cars and would not take a Porsche as a gift, but at least I know a little of the language. I remember a sports car freak telling me his car had been giving him trouble so he scrubbed the tappets with a wire brush. I believe that cars no longer have tappets, and I have forgotten what they were, but at the time I was able to put on a show of interest and make an intelligent observation.

After a few weeks we POs were sent off to a WOSBI, which means a War Office Selection Board Interview. This was to see if we were fit to be turned from Potential into Actual officers. I passed, but I ought to have failed. Most of it was pretty simple, in the way of intelligence tests, essay writing and giving a five-minute talk called a lecturette, but there was a practical test which should have told them that I was not the sort of person they were looking for. I cannot be certain as to the details, but, roughly speaking, they put two parallel ropes on the ground about four yards apart which, they said, represented the banks of a bottomless chasm. I, on one side, was given the task of getting five men and three barrels to the other side, using a couple of impossibly small planks and a piece of rope which was too short to reach the further bank. Other people managed to do this, but to me it was impossible, and when the allotted time ran out we were still on the wrong side of the chasm. Nevertheless I passed, which I can only assume was because I shouted a lot. I thought that they wanted to know if I had leadership qualities, and my experience of the army suggested that the way to display leadership qualities was to shout a lot, so I did, and that must have done it. A possible factor was that the army at the time seemed to have a superstitious belief that anyone who had passed through Oxford or Cambridge must inevitably have the makings of a successful officer. The idea that a man who could stroke an eight and tell you the date of the Battle of Marathon might be incapable of reading a map was entirely foreign to them. The same superstition prevailed when I first arrived at my regiment, but in the course of time I managed to dispel it.

To be made into an officer I was sent to Mons officer cadet school, near Aldershot, which was ruled by the famous RSM Brittan, about whom there are many stories. He liked to bully junior officers, and once spotted a young man walking with his parents beside the barrack square, immediately after a passing out parade. Brittan saluted him, but the young man did not notice, and did not return the salute, so Brittan roared at him, "I'm saluting you sir!"

Back across the barrack square, in the languid tones appropriate to a newly-commissioned cavalry officer, came floating the reply, "And so you should be, Mr Brittan, so you should be."

We did a lot more infantry training, including rifle drill, although they did not have rifles in the Armoured Corps but pistols or Sten guns. I once came on parade with my rifle sling upside down, which is an easy mistake to make if you are in a hurry. The adjutant, who was from the Life Guards, passed by with his mind on other things, but it did not escape the eye of Brittan.

"Look at that officer cadet sir. Look at his rifle sling!"

The adjutant eyed me as if I was an interesting specimen. "Oh yes," he said.

"Shall I charge him, sir?"

"Oh, yes."

"Take his name!" roared Brittan, whereat a drill sergeant stabbed me in the back with his pace stick.

"Your name, sir?"

"Officer Cadet Enfield, sir."

"You've lost your name, sir."

I always liked that particular bit of army logic. If something is taken, then whoever had it before has it no longer, and as the sergeant had taken my name, it followed absolutely that I must have lost it.

In the intervals of drill and polishing they taught us useful things like map reading, wireless procedure and military law. They took us to a range and let us fire the gun of a tank. Then after four months they graded us A, B, or (in my case) C, and after a final parade, sent us off to our regiments.

*

The Eighth Kings Royal Irish Hussars when I joined was stationed in Germany at Lüneberg. It was, as the name suggests, an Irish regiment, but the number of Irishmen in the British army varies from time to time, and as Englishmen had to do National Service while Irishmen did not, there were only a few Irishmen in the Eighth Hussars. They kept up the regimental Irishness by putting the officers into green hats embroidered with gold shamrocks and calling the squadrons R, B and C. R squadron was spelt A squadron but pronounced R as Irishmen are supposed to be unable to say A and always say R, or AH, as you prefer.

They also had a lot of horses, and keeping horses is an Irish trait alright, but in this case it was more to do with being a cavalry regiment, and they certainly did not have more horses than their predecessors, the Royal Scots Greys. The Eighth Hussars, when posted to Germany to relieve the Greys, took over the barracks, the tanks and the horses. The tanks were found to be in rather bad condition, and it was explained that, "Greys don't like starting the tanks, as it frightens the horses."

The horses were kept purely for pleasure and not for any military or ceremonial purpose. They were looked after by a mixture of German grooms who were on the payroll as clerks and storemen, and Eighth Hussars troopers. There are those who argue for the return of National Service on account of the moral uplift it conveyed which, for those who spent two years of service to Queen and country in mucking out the horses ridden by the officers of the Eighth Hussars, may not have been very great.

The horses were one of the good parts of my service. There were lots of them, paid for by the army and we could ride as much as we liked for nothing, so we did, twice a day, morning and evening. There was a Prussian count who had lost his estates in East Prussia, and he, too, was on the payroll as a clerk, but employed as a riding master. He was an excellent instructor, and under his guidance I got to be good enough to ride in a point-to-point without falling off. The other good part was the mess life. I have read that some regiments were a bit unpleasant to National Service officers, but the Eighth Hussars were as friendly as anything. They lived in even better style than I had enjoyed at Oxford. The German army had built barracks for a Panzer regiment with excellent accommodations for officers and superb stabling for horses, and we were now in it. My days of polishing were over as I had a batman who did it for me. The food was excellent, with a mess sergeant in charge and mess waiters in attendance, and most of all I liked the mess nights.

*

Cavalry officers love dressing up. When I was commissioned I got a uniform allowance and a letter from the adjutant telling me to go to the regimental tailor in Hanover Square for my mess kit, to Herbert Johnson in Bond Street for my green hat and for a soft brown hat, and to Locks in St James Street for a hard bowler hat. The tailor fitted me up with a blue patrol jacket with embossed brass buttons and chain mail on the shoulders, a pair of tight blue trousers called overalls, patent leather boots called wellingtons and a pair of spurs. On mess nights we put on the whole lot and came strutting into the mess with chainmail going clink-clink and spurs going jingle-jingle. On such nights the table was laid out with a wealth of race cups, statuettes and other regimental silver, the regimental band played in an ante-room and we got a superb meal. After dinner there were sometimes games, and the night I remember best involved a boffin.

He was a boffin who had been sent to stay with us by the War Office as he wanted to study some aspect of the gun on the Centurion tank. He was small, middle aged and unassuming, and as the Eighth Hussars had very good manners we did our best to make him welcome, but all the same we rather looked down on him. He put that right on the mess night.

We all came into the mess going clink-clink, jingle-jingle, and he slipped quietly in, wearing a dinner jacket, as was proper. When the games started he watched for a time, and then said, "Try this".

He took a big stuffed armchair and put it on its back, with the seat sticking up towards the ceiling. Then he pushed another chair up to it which he left upright. After that he walked to the far end of the mess, ran forward, jumped over the upright chair and hit the seat of the second chair with his bottom, which knocked it upright, so that he ended sitting comfortably in the chair which had previously been flat on its back.

We looked at him with alarm. My first thought was that if I tried it I would probably catch my spurs in the first chair and break my neck. To gain time, someone said "Could you just do it again?"

"Certainly," and he did.

There was a pause, but the honour of the regiment was at stake, and we could not just funk it. The situation was saved, typically, by Richard Dill, then a major. Richard was Irish, rich, good looking, a superb horseman, very witty, had served in the Normandy campaign and, to add a final touch to this particular occasion, had broken his collarbone in a steeple chase and had his arm in a sling. It was Richard who marched to the far end of the mess, turned, charged forward, flew triumphantly over the first chair and found himself sitting safely in the second chair, broken collarbone and all. After that it was up to the rest of us - some did it, some didn't, and I'm proud to say that I was one who did. As for the boffin, we realised that he was a fine fellow, took him to our bosoms and hoped he would come again.

There was a snag to mess nights. The rule was that no junior officer might leave the mess before the last guest was gone. This could mean that some boozy brigadier from brigade HQ would be standing in front of the fire with a whisky in his hand, so happy to be back in a regimental mess that he had no wish to leave, while we young fellows who had to be up at six in the morning to ride horses would be knocking billiard balls about the table and stifling our yawns, longing for him to go so that we could get a few hours sleep.

As part of the dressing-up business I had dutifully bought a hard bowler hat and a soft brown hat, which formed part of a sort of out-of-uniform uniform. The bowler, as well as for use when riding a horse, was to be worn on leave in London with a grey suit, stiff collar, gloves and umbrella. Guards officers dressed in the same way, and guardsmen were supposed to salute their officers out of uniform, but they could not always recognise them. As a result, if you went near one of their sentry boxes, the man eyed you anxiously, and if you gave him a nod, you got a crashing salute. Then the proper thing was to raise your bowler hat and say either, "Good morning" or "Good afternoon." The soft hat was for such occasions as a point-to-point or Hanover races. Richard Dill, who was always good for an anecdote, once came back from leave and said, "I ran into Billy Richardson in London. He said he was *sneaking about in a soft hat and collar, trying to pretend he was only passing through.*"

While living this life I had a brief encounter with the Duke of Edinburgh. To the great delight of the regiment, he became its Colonel-in-Chief, and came to see us. We prepared in much the same way as for the visit of the CIGS at Catterick, which is to say that we practised marching round the barrack square with the band playing, and when the day came we put on our best boots and did it while he watched. He did not make a speech, like the Field Marshall, but he paid a visit to the sergeants' mess, then to the stables, and then came to the officers' mess for lunch. We stood in a line round the walls, and the colonel presented us individually to his Royal Highness. When it came to my turn, it went like this:

Colonel: "This is Edward Enfield. He has come to us from Oxford. We are all trying to persuade him to become a regular soldier."

HRH: "Can't you sit on his head until he does?

Me: Indeed, sir, that's exactly what they do."

HRH: "Ha ha ha."

I might well have become a regular soldier had it not been for the beastly soldiering. They made me a troop leader, which meant that I was in charge of three tanks, a sergeant, a corporal and nine troopers. When we were in barracks it was nothing worse than boring. The rest of the troop busied themselves somehow, by greasing bits of the tanks or hosing the things down, while I either watched or wandered about in an aimless manner. It was when we went out of barracks that things went wrong.

The colonel, who had fought in France, been a prisoner of war, and commanded the regiment in Korea, wrote in the regimental magazine that, "We soon discovered that peacetime schemes in the British Army of the Rhine bore no resemblance to any other form of warfare." Possibly I might have managed better in the real sort, though I doubt it, but anyway I was hopeless at the BAOR training exercises.

My greatest difficulty was in reading a map. Those who think map-reading is a matter of finding your way along roads where there are signposts and through villages which have their names on display, have no idea of what it is like on Lüneberg Heath, where there are no roads, no signposts and nothing to steer on but contours. To others these contours were full of meaning and seemed to be as good as signposts, but to me they meant nothing, so I was constantly lost. The proper way to deal with an officer like that is to give him a sergeant who can read a map, but unfortunately my sergeant was as hopeless as I was, so whenever we trundled out onto the heath we were very quickly lost. On my first exercise I lost not only my troop but the whole squadron. I have mentioned the army's superstitious belief that an Oxford graduate must be a capable soldier, and, relying on this, the squadron leader chose my troop to lead C squadron from barracks to the training area. It was, of all things, a night exercise, so we set off in the dark, and of course I got lost, with the rest of the squadron trailing along behind in the belief that I knew where I was going. Eventually someone realised that we were in quite the wrong place and somehow found a way to get us to the right one, where the other squadrons were waiting and wondering where we had got to, as they all went straight there without any difficulty.

When we were playing war games in the training area they used to ring me up on the wireless and say "Hello Three - where are you? Over." To this I would reply "Three - wait. Out." Then I would take a guess at where I might possibly be, turn the map reference into the code for the day (designed to deceive the Russians who were supposed to be listening) and say, "Hello Three. I am at Able Jig Charlie Baker Dog Oboe - over." To this they always seemed to start in the same way: "Three - you *can't* be." Then they would add some unanswerable supporting argument such as, "If you were there we could see you", or "That's where *we* are", or something else equally damning.

I prefer to draw a veil over my exploits in the field, but I will just comment on one of the peculiarities of the wireless procedure of the time. It would have been a breach of security to use words like infantry, squadron or tanks, as this would have given the game away to the listening Russians, so we used circumlocutions which were supposed to put them off the scent. I remember one gunner officer who had somehow got onto our wireless net reporting that, "Our little friends are all around us, but they are not worried as your big boys are here to look after them." I imagined Boris and Ivan scratching their heads and saying, "What is meaning - little friend? What is big boys?" but as the infantry were always referred to as "our little friends" they must have understood perfectly, and he might as well have said infantry and tanks.

Mercifully, at the end of my first summer they made me Assistant Adjutant, which limited my capacity for harm as I didn't have to go out of barracks any more. My two year stint came to a pleasant end, and I had to look for a job. This was, to use the current phrase, a watershed. I regard school, Oxford and the army as my education, and after that life began.

*

One of the many differences between that time and this is that, when I started work, almost everyone I worked for or with had been in one of the services, and most of them in the army. It is impossible to say what difference it makes that this is no longer true, but it must have made *some* difference. National Service was certainly a toss-up, and spending two years as a clerk in the Pay Corps or as an officer's batman, as happened to some, cannot have done anyone much good. On the other hand, if you were lucky it gave you something to look back on with pleasure and amusement. In my Oxford summer vacations when I was helping to get the corn in, there would sometimes be a break while we waited for the next wagon, and then the conversation would not be about wireless or football, but more often the waiting farmhands would reminisce about their time spent in the forces, in Cairo or Germany or Athens. I expect that Alec Alan the Scottish farm boy, if he was, say, a tank driver in Germany, thinks back to his service in the same way and feels glad to have done it. As, for all my deficiencies, am I.

Chapter 6

How I Got the Job

I came to work for John Swire & Sons more or less by accident. While on leave, I went for an interview at the Oxford University Appointments Board, where I filled in a form which included the question, "Would you be willing to spend your working life abroad?" To this I answered firmly, "No." This set off a flow of possible jobs with, I think, a factory in Blackburn at £450 a year, or perhaps it was a foundry in Bootle at something similar. I did actually go for an interview with a job which offered £500 at the Mac Fisheries, but there a man in a terrible suit and rimless glasses managed altogether to put me off the idea of working for them. Then, presumably by mistake, someone at the Appointments Board sent me the details of a job with John Swire & Sons and, as they operated solely in the Far East and Australia, this would certainly require me to spend my working life abroad.

The salary was princely - £1,000 a year to start, and the Swire document painted an enticing picture of life in Hong Kong, Japan and Bangkok. Memory plays strange tricks, and the letter cannot possibly have talked about pheasant shooting on the Yangtze Kiang, but somehow I have it in my mind that there was something along those lines. What settled the matter, though, was the fact that my regiment, before I joined, had been in the Korean war, in the thick of the battle of the Imjin river with Chinese soldiers swarming over their tanks and trying to give them hand grenades to share among the crew. When not so engaged, they had gone to Japan on leave, where I gathered that many of them had had a lovely time among the girls who worked in the bars of Tokyo and Yokohama. The general opinion of the unmarried officers who had had that experience was that I should certainly try to get myself taken on, and once established, I should get the rest of them into the firm as well. So I applied, taking this momentous step at the urging of my brother officers in the Eighth Kings Royal Irish Hussars.

I was asked to come to the Swires' London office, and there I was interviewed by Mr J. K. Swire, the head of the firm, and Sir John Masson, who I later learnt had been knighted for services to shipping during the war. I only remember two questions, the first of which was from Mr Swire, who said, "You didn't get a first, did you?"

"Only a second" I replied.

He nodded approvingly. "I tend to distrust a man who gets a first," he said. I could only suppose that they had once had an unfortunate experience with a man of exceptional brilliance, but Mr Swire did not elaborate, and I did not like to enquire. The second question was posed at the City of London Club where they took me to lunch, and it was "What would you like to drink?" I wondered if this was some sort of test, like giving cherry pie to candidates for the Foreign Office to see whether they spat the stones into their spoons, or straight onto their plates (or, as in the case of one terrified young man, whether they swallowed the lot.) Anyway, I was not the sort of chap who says, "I believe the '52 Beaujolais is now at its best," so I asked for a pint of bitter, and as I was offered a job that must have been all right.

I accepted, and between the time that I was demobbed and the time they wanted me to leave for Hong Kong there was a space of about 4 weeks. One of the things I did in this time was to lay down some wine.

This needs a bit of explaining. I was no great wine bibber, as I have said. Wine was not then drunk in the quantities that it is now, and Christmas was the only time we had it at home. At Oxford I drank it only at meetings of the Shakespeare Society (always known as the Shaker) but not otherwise. This society met once a term, in a room in college set aside for the evening. We gathered in our dinner jackets, the college chef served up an excellent dinner and the president laid on the best wines he thought we could afford. Then, after we had drunk the Queen's health in a glass of port at the end of dinner, the president would rise to his feet and say with all solemnity: "Gentlemen, I move that the Bard be not read tonight." As this was always carried nem. con. The Bard never was read at meetings of the Shakespeare Society and the members carried on drinking.

In the army we drank wine on mess nights and I swallowed it happily enough without thinking anything about it. However, the idea of laying down wine was in the air. People talked about it and in particular they talked of laying down port for their old age. It seemed to me that this would be a good way for me to dispose of some of the enormous salary which John Swire & Sons were about to shower upon me. I suppose that my annual £1,000 must be equivalent to something like £40,000 today. It seemed to me to be such a huge amount that I would never get through it all, so I had better use some of it to lay down some port. Accordingly, I applied to Harveys of Bristol.

You can still buy Harvey's Bristol Cream, but the firm of Harveys of Bristol is now part of some conglomerate. In those days it was an independent company, and it was from them that my Oxford college used to buy its wines. On the strength of this, aged 24, I went into their London office in St. James's Street and explained that I was going out to the Far East and I wished to lay down some port to the value of £25. I proposed that they should keep it for me in their Bristol cellars until it was ready to drink, and I would give them a pound a month until the £25 was paid off.

This may sound a daft idea but it isn't if you multiply by 40. Looked at like that, the £25 that I was proposing to pay out would now be worth £1,000, and I would be paying it off in just over 2 years at the rate of £40 a month. Nothing wrong with that, you might think. Anyway, whoever I spoke to could see nothing wrong at all. On the contrary, he thought it was such a brilliant idea that I ought to speak to one of the directors, and I was shown in to see Mr Harry Waugh. His name was new to me, but I have since learnt that it was one to conjure with in the wine trade, and that he was an expert of the first order. He was also extremely nice and hugely enthusiastic, but, he said, "You should not just have port. You ought to have some red wine as well. Do you prefer claret or Burgundy?"

"Claret," I said, not able to tell one from the other but thinking it sounded smarter.

"Oh, I am so glad," said Mr Waugh. "I find most young people nowadays prefer Burgundy."

"Not me," said I, generally giving him to understand that I was a claret man.

Mr Waugh then got out some lists and started hopping about in a state of excitement. He quickly disposed of the port, to the extent of half a dozen bottles, and then went on to the claret. He kept consulting me on matters on which I had no opinion, saying things like, "What would you say to a couple of the Calon Ségur?"

"Splendid!" I would reply.

"Why don't we have a magnum of the Château Talbot?"

"Why not, indeed!"

And so we went on till my £25 was fully allocated, after which I went off to Hong Kong.

For years afterwards Harveys used to write to me annually telling me how my wine was getting along. One year they would say it was "keeping well" and the next year that it was "maturing nicely." They went on with variations on this theme, through "still wants keeping" and "coming along well" till they began to sound a more exciting note by saying, "ready soon." Finally we reached the point when they said "ready now."

What wine was it? you may wonder. Apart from the two Châteaux that I have mentioned, the names I seem to remember are Château Léoville Barton and Château Cheval Blanc. I think there were vintages of 2 different years, one of which was certainly 1948, and this I have read was a particularly brilliant year. I am confident that under the guidance of Mr Harry Waugh I was in possession, had I but realised it, of a small collection of the best wine that money could buy.

I did not realise it, though, in the monetary sense. If I had let it lie in Harvey's cellars until those vintages became extremely rare and greatly sought after I could have turned it all into money and it would have been the best investment I have ever made in my life. I didn't though, we simply drank it, and while it was certainly very delicious I did not realise, in the other sense, just how good it was until the night Peter Wagner came to dinner. Peter raised his glass to his nose, sniffed and said "Claret, by the smell."

Then he tasted it, and said, "Oh, this is something special".

Then he took another sip and said "I think it is the 1948" (which it was) and then he named the château correctly.

I had heard of people who were able to do these things, but I had never met one. Now that I knew that Peter was such a person I reserved whatever remained of the original stock for nights when he was going to be there. This was all some years after we had left the East and were living in England with a modest salary, a mortgage, two children and a tight budget. Nevertheless, if you came to dinner with the Enfields on a night when Peter Wagner was present, you were given wines which would have graced the table of a multimillionaire.

Having made these arrangements for the future, I flew to Hong Kong, an undertaking which gave me a mild grudge from which I never quite recovered. In flying out I was pioneering. I discovered later that everyone who had joined before me, and at least one person who joined after me, came out by sea, but it was arranged that I should come by air.

I had never flown before, and it was horrible. I flew by the now defunct Pan American Airways and I think the journey was meant to take 36 hours but took longer because somewhere between London and Frankfurt one of the engines started spitting out oil and we had to go back to get it fixed. In those days the planes had to keep landing to refuel, and so we stopped at Frankfurt, Beirut, Karachi, Calcutta and Rangoon before we got to Hong Kong. At every stop we had to get off and troop into the airport terminal, where we sat for an hour while they took on fuel. The airline seats of those days were much like airline seats now, pretty uncomfortable after a time, and if you did manage to drop off to sleep you were likely to be woken by a Pan Am airhostess leaning over you and shouting in your ear, "Hot chocolate?" From this I emerged into the heat of Hong Kong dazed, exhausted and unwashed.

Part of my grudge was that those who came by sea had enjoyed a cruise of some 5 weeks living in luxury and going ashore at interesting places such as Colombo, so I felt hard done by. This, however, was the minor part of the grudge, the greater part being a matter of money. They who came by sea were paid from the moment they stepped on board, so they accumulated 5 weeks salary while living the highlife with nothing to pay for but their drinks. I was paid from the day I got on the plane, and having started with nothing I arrived with nothing, but was faced with expenses. I had, for a start, to eat, and I had to buy some tropical clothes, so they gave me an advance on my first month's pay which they clawed back in the second month. I don't think I ever quite recovered. I don't know how it was but in all the years that I worked in the Far East, whether married or single, I never seemed to be at all flush of money. It must have been something to do with me. I never owned a car, although other people did. I did not gamble furiously at the races or drink heavily, or fritter away my money on loose women, but I never seemed to be at all well off. Perhaps if I had come by sea I would have got ahead and stayed ahead.

Chapter 7

Hong Kong – The Job

"Little else is required to carry a State to the highest degree of opulence from the lowest barbarism but peace, easy taxes and a tolerable administration of justice" – Adam Smith, quoted in the Daily Telegraph January 2005.

I have never read The Wealth of Nations and do not suppose that I ever shall. This is partly because it comes as a thick and daunting volume which I might never get through, but mainly because the sentence quoted above seems to say all that is necessary and I see no need to look further. Apart from anything else it explains the great success of the British Empire.

One is not supposed to say anything pleasant about the British Empire nowadays. The proper thing is to wallow in the horrors of the African slave trade as if we invented it, which we didn't, and as if we had a monopoly of it, which we hadn't, and to disregard the fact that we put a stop to it, which we did. In the heyday of the Empire, the army kept the peace, and the judges, magistrates and district officers administered a system of justice which was generally rather better than tolerable as they were usually both fair and incorruptible. I do not know whether the taxes paid by Africans and Indians could reasonably be described as easy, but I cannot believe that they approached the rapacious levels now levied in Britain. However disreputable the means by which we acquired an Empire, and however disagreeable the British may have made themselves socially, and however much the subject nations might have resented being ruled by foreigners, it can hardly be denied that the effect, particularly in Africa, was to carry a number of peoples to a situation of considerable prosperity.

I make these interesting comments as a preliminary to saying that the Adam Smith dictum was entirely true of the British Crown Colony of Hong Kong in 1954. There was no war; the British were administering justice in a tolerable manner, and income tax was never more than half a crown in the pound, otherwise 12½%. The effect, in this barren lump of rock with its few leased extra acres, was to produce such a degree of opulence that the governor was obliged to close the border with China in order to hold back the vast numbers who wished to flood in from the communist paradise on the other side. And let it not be forgotten that most of the Chinese of Hong Kong would have liked to have been left as they were, rather than handed over to the Chinese of the mainland. When the time came to lower the Union flag there were many who held British passports and asked to be allowed to emigrate to Britain, but this was refused – a great mistake in my view. They should been allowed to come provided they lived north of the Watford Gap, and then these industrious people with a penchant for living in tower blocks would have revitalised the north of England and created an opulent state of affairs up there. But, as so often, the people in charge did not think of consulting me, and so the chance was lost.

In Hong Kong I was put to work in a big open plan office with overhead fans which blew the papers off one's desk in the heat of summer. Behind me sat a man called Jock Campbell and behind him, in a glass box, was Trevor Knight. Trevor's title was Hong Kong Agent, and Jock and I made up the rest of his European staff, everyone else being Chinese. The prevailing noise was the clattering of abacuses as the clerks all around the office did rapid calculations to do with freight rates for ships' cargoes.

Without doubt the abacus must have been swept away long ago, replaced first of all by the battery-operated calculator, and after that by the computer. I expect that in those days Chinese children must all have had abacus lessons at school, as all the Chinese staff could use one to make the most complicated calculations in a short time and with a loud noise. Also, if I said to one of them, "What are six sevens?" his right hand would reach out to his abacus and go rattle rattle, before he answered "forty two."

Possibly the abacus is one of the reasons why the Chinese are so terribly clever. The cleverness of the Chinese is a subject which has long interested me, and I believe it comes about because they have a way of making things difficult for themselves, and then the business of overcoming these difficulties stretches their brains to such an extent that they end up terribly clever. This must apply above all to their extraordinarily complicated language and their bizarre method of writing it. Very likely working an abacus is also difficult, and now that they have given it up the Chinese may become slightly less clever than they were before.

John Swire and Sons traded in Hong Kong as "Butterfield and Swire," and although there was no trace of a surviving Butterfield, the firm was commonly referred to as "Butterfields" and their office as the Butterfield building. It was a fine old two-storey brick construction separated from the harbour by a road. There were many such buildings in Hong Kong, and nearly all, if not all, have been pulled down and replaced with skyscrapers. A few right-minded people once formed themselves into a group called something like the Hong Kong Preservation Society, hoping to save some examples of prime colonial architecture from destruction, but they might as well have called themselves the Canute Society, as they were powerless to prevent the relentless tide of money from sweeping away all such anachronisms.

I worked for the Swires, in one way and another, for five years and I never, ever in my later life came across any organisation that came anywhere near them for effortless efficiency. I now realise that it is truly remarkable that, in all my time, I never once went to a meeting, or was unable to talk to someone because that person was in a meeting. If they wanted to talk to each other, they just walked to each other's offices or desks and talked. Everyone kept strictly to office hours and no one took work home or let the business impinge upon their weekends. There was no feeling of frantic effort, and yet everything got done and everything seemed to prosper. The key, I believe, was that all the money belonged to real people, some of whom one could identify, such as the Mr J. K. Swire who had interviewed me in London. If you went out and made a few extra Hong Kong dollars, then some real person somewhere, probably called Swire, was a bit better off. There was, of course, no fancy management talk; the people were people, not Human Resources, and there were no bonuses because there didn't need to be, as everything went with a swing without them.

I, as the most junior person in the whole show, was taken in hand by the man who sat on my left, whose name was Tsoi Ning. It was odd that he only had two names, as the Chinese usually have three, and they put them back to front. By this I mean that Mao Tse Tung was Chairman Mao and Chiang Kai Shek was Generalissimo Chiang. If you had been on intimate terms with either of them, you would have used their last two names, saying things like, "Good morning, Tse Tung" or "How are you, Kai Shek?" Tsoi Ning seemed to be at a disadvantage, having only two names, but it didn't matter as he was usually just called Tsoi. By contrast, the name of the man who sat on my right was Mok Hing Kong, and as he was a senior clerk and a venerable figure, he was always called Mr Mok.

Tsoi Ning looked to be about the same age as I, but I discovered that he was a married man with two children, so he must have been a bit older. Officially he was the shorthand typist and took dictation, but he extended his duties beyond that with the general intention of keeping things going smoothly. As soon as he and I were introduced he set about fixing me up with a Chinese name.

In Hong Kong, and in Bangkok later, I always had a business card with my name in English on one side and in Chinese on the other. This was a matter to which Tsoi Ning gave immediate attention. He explained to me that the junior clerks and office boys had a mischievous way of taking an English name and turning it into something Chinese that was disrespectful, or even rude, and he wanted to get in before they did. The only example he gave me was of a man called Meffan, whose name had been turned into Muk Faan, which meant oatmeal. I could see no particular difficulty in his being Mr Oatmeal, but Tsoi Ning didn't think much of it and wanted something better for me. After trying a variety of sounds in Cantonese to get an equivalent to Enfield, he decided that I should be Mr On Fey Lo, which he said meant Safe Air Travel. The Lo bit, meaning travel, was not really necessary, as On Fey by itself is closer to Enfield, but for me to be Mr Safe Air somehow failed to suit Tsoi Ning, so he added the third element. This was prophetic. I could hardly have had a better name when the time came for me to transfer to Cathay Pacific Airways in Thailand. For any member of the Chinese community flying in or out of Bangkok, to have Mr Safe Air Travel in charge was bound to inspire confidence.

In this connection I will tell you that, sometime later and to my enormous pleasure, I made a joke in Cantonese. I knew very few words in that language, but a new recruit arrived from England whose name was Forsyth. "Ah," I said to Tsoi Ning. "Mr Foh Tsai," which is the Chinese for matches, as in a box of matches. Tsoi Ning thought this was such an exquisite jest that he left his desk and walked over to Mr Mok Hing Kong and poured out a flood of Cantonese in which I could distinguish the words On Fey Lo, Forsyth, and Foh Tsai. Mr Mok dignified my witticism with a quiet smile, after which Tsoi Ning walked to the desk of another of the clerks and went through it all again. This time the clerk laughed openly, where after Tsoi Ning went back to his own desk and the second clerk got up and walked to the desk of a third clerk and told the joke to him. So it went on, and I could hear my little witticism working its way all around the office to the sound of happy laughter.

My principal duties were to meet and dispatch the ships of the China Navigation Company, to write letters to the captains of these ships, and to sign bills of lading. A bill of lading is in effect a receipt to say that the items specified are on board the ship. I must have signed thousands of them, which was rather like being chairman of the Bank of England signing bank notes individually, because once they had my signature on them they could be exchanged for money by whoever was sending the goods off. They further entitled someone else to receive the goods at the port of destination.

It was Tsoi Ning who taught me how to write the letters to the captains, which he could perfectly well have written himself instead of taking them down at my dictation. The content was pretty well standard. It was a matter of telling the captain what cargo had been booked to be loaded in Hong Kong, where he was to go next, when he was to sail, and when the fuel he had asked for would be delivered. If I managed to make a mistake, Tsoi Ning would put down his pencil and say firmly "No!" and the only time I got one past him was when I contrived to order 140 tons of coal to be delivered to a ship that ran on oil.

All the captains could navigate, which of course was essential, but seemed to me to be remarkable nonetheless. There was one who had the reputation of being both inefficient and a drunk, to whom I wrote one of my letters saying he was to go to Zamboanga and load timber. "Where's Zamboanga?" he asked.

"I think it's in the Philippines" I said. He just grunted, but two days later he steamed away and ten days after that he sent a telegram saying,

"Arrived Zamboanga". I thought that was extremely clever. He had never heard of the place before, but among all that cluster of little islands which make up the Philippines he found it straight away, on the first attempt. Had it been me I would have had to go to Manila and ask for directions.

Every ship coming to Hong Kong sent a telegram with a brief summary of the cargo to be discharged, and two of the more interesting cargoes were buffaloes and White Russians. The buffaloes travelled on deck from Bangkok, big patient animals that had to be lifted high in the air one at a time on a sling attached to a crane, and then lowered into a lighter to be taken ashore. The White Russians came from China, and went ashore in an Immigration Department launch.

China at that time was said to be closed. People could not go there from Hong Kong or anywhere else, but ships could load at certain ports, and ours used regularly to call at Tientsien and Shanghai on their way south from Japan. When Red Russians took over Russia, a lot of White Russians escaped to China, and when Red Chinese took over China, the White Russians needed to move again. They used to arrive in Hong Kong in batches of about twelve, evidently destitute, the men wearing baggy suits and clutching cardboard suitcases tied with string, and the women equally shabby. Their faces seemed to have no expressions, so they looked like the classic refugees that they were. Once ashore they were, I think, absorbed into the small Russian community of Hong Kong. I suppose they were lucky, but I still felt sorry for them, as I did for the buffaloes, which were not lucky but were on their way to the slaughterhouse.

At first I lived in the Butterfield's bachelor mess, in a fine old house at the top of Victoria Peak, as high above the main city as it was possible to get. It was often shrouded in mist, with a consequent risk of clothes and books going mouldy. Life was a mixture of the luxurious and the Spartan. There were four or five of us, and we never had to lift a finger by way of looking after ourselves. When you undressed at night you threw your clothes into a corner and next day they were carried off, washed, ironed and returned. In summer we wore white cotton trousers, and these went into the corner every day along with everything else. We made no beds, we washed no dishes, everything was done for us.

The staff consisted of an elderly Chinese man whose name was Lee but whom we sometimes addressed as "Boy" because his title was "cook-boy". He addressed us, rather embarrassingly, as "Master". He cooked us breakfast, and dinner if we wanted it. His wife was the amah who did the washing and there was a "coolie-boy" who probably came in for quite a lot of work, without our knowing what he did. We paid no rent and we were left to settle our living expenses with Lee. He kept a record in a notebook of everything he spent, and he once charged us rather a lot for One Iron Ball, so we queried it and it turned out to be an ironing board. On the other hand, when he wanted to be recompensed for Three Thirsk Riges we let it go, as they only cost 20 cents each, whatever they may have been.

All this made for easy living, but the accommodation was sparse. The house, being old, had a lot of well-established and healthy cockroaches which scuttled about but did no harm. We each had a room with a bed, table, chair and cupboard, and that was it. We shared two bathrooms, and there was a recurrent water shortage every summer. When that happened the water went off altogether, except for two hours every other day. To cope with that the baths had to be filled when the taps were running and the water made to last until it came on again at the main.

We ate in the large entry hall, and there was no sitting room. We had no bar, we stocked no drink so we could not entertain, and truthfully Lee's cooking was not such as one would wish to offer to a guest.

There was no pidgin English spoken in the office, but ships' captains used it freely. "You talkee every man come catchee money" was the sort of thing a captain would say to the steward when he wanted to pay the crew. Cook-boys and amahs used it a lot. "I am going to town to buy the dinner. Would you like chicken?" became "My go town-side catchee dinner. Master likee chicken?" to which you might reply, "My thinkee fish more better." The word "pidgin" itself could be used to convey an abstract idea. "A very fine view" would be "Plenty look-see pidgin." My boss, Trevor Knight, was dead against this sort of talk. He was a Mandarin speaker with a high regard for the Chinese and he though it unfair to talk in this foolish gibberish, as it gave them no chance to improve their English. I am sure he was right, and it would have been much better to say, "Why are you here?" rather than, "What for you come thisee place?" but the habit was catching.

After a time I was moved to the Duty Mess in a modern flat lower down the Peak. There life was better. There was a much better cook-boy who served much better meals, and though we kept no stock of drink we got some in if we decided to entertain. Our guests were usually given pheasant, a Chinese bird which was very plentiful and so did not cost much, which we liked. There were three of us, and the Duty part of it meant that one of us had to be there at all times in case some ship sent a telegram which had to be dealt with straight away. Ships do not keep office hours and are no respecters of weekends or holidays, so such a telegram might come at any moment.

The one I remember best was sent because, on a later voyage, the same captain whom I dispatched to Zamboanga got drunk in Shanghai and pulled the pigtail of a Chinese girl interpreter. A senior Chinese official came and protested, and I suppose he must have had horn-rimmed glasses because the captain told him he was a goggle-eyed twit. This was the story which eventually came out, but the telegram just said that the Chinese authorities were refusing to let the ship sail and negotiations were in progress.

It took two days to sort it out. The Chinese wanted an apology, and they drafted one which was couched in such abject terms of grovelling humility that the captain refused to sign it. He countered by writing on a piece of paper, "I am sorry I called your man a goggle-eyed twit" and proffered that, but the offensive brevity made things worse. The ship was stuck there with neither party prepared to give way, and I think in the end the captain was told by Head Office to swallow his pride and sign whatever they wanted provided they would let the ship go.

There was one captain called Willie Hargreaves who told me that in his earlier days he had been captured by pirates. Now that the Somali pirates are so active this is not all that uncommon, but in the 1950s there were not many men who could tell of such a thing. Before the war, pirates on the China coast used to come on board as deck passengers and then, when at sea, rise up, overpower the officers and run the ship ashore. They usually just stole the cargo and any valuables, but this time they took the officers as well and tried to hold them to ransom. The Swires of those days were men of principle and thought that the idea of buying their officers back from a bunch of pirates was a very bad principle indeed. On this point they stood firm, and would not offer a single Hong

Kong dollar. This was all right for them, but not so good for Willie Hargreaves, who was afraid that the pirates might start sending him back in instalments, putting one of his ears or fingers in the post as a way of raising the stakes. They didn't though. After leading him around the China coast on the end of a rope for 3 months, they got bored and let him go.

After a time I was given the job of sorting out the hawkers. The fleet was made up of ships which were basically cargo carriers but most of them had cabins for ten or twelve people in all, and there were two ships which could accommodate seventy. Travelling round on cargo boats was popular in an era when cruise ships were rare, so there were almost always tourists on board. As soon as the ship tied up and lowered its gangway a swarm of hawkers dashed on board, - shirtmakers, tailors, moneychangers, jewellers, sellers of curios, old ladies with lace tablecloths and possibly others that I have forgotten. On the whole the tourists liked it. It was an opportunity to haggle and strike bargains without the trouble of carrying stuff back from the shops ashore, and in your cabin you could be measured and fitted for a suit or a dress which would be finished and delivered before the ship sailed, even if it was only in port for 48 hours. The hawkers got out of hand, however. There were so many of them that they got all over the ship and the tourists felt pestered and threatened, so I was told to cut the number down to two of each sort.

I made a list of the different types of hawker, got some passes made, and asked the stevedores to put the word out that anyone who wanted a pass was to apply to me, and without such a pass they could no longer come aboard our ships. They arrived in the office in droves. I issued passes on a first come first served basis, and the lucky ones had to take theirs away and bring them back having stuck on a photograph of themselves, after which I would graciously sign them. The unlucky ones made a dreadful fuss, but I sternly repelled them, except for one old lady who wept so bitterly that I invented a new category of hawker specially for her, as a means of saving her from impending starvation without compromising the principle.

It seemed to work quite well, and the number of hawkers was sensibly diminished, but there were terrible scenes at Christmas, for which I was not prepared. The word "kum-shaw" when used on its own means something worth having that you get from someone else at no cost to yourself. A DVD that comes with the newspaper could be described as a bit of kum-shaw, or if you bought a leg of lamb and the butcher threw in some sausages, you could say that you got some kum-shaw sausages. When combined with Christmas, it takes on a special meaning. I presume that there is a Chinese custom by which, at a certain time of year, there has to be a giving of presents between people who are engaged in business. The presents only flow in one direction, which is, so to speak, upwards. If you passed to someone a bit of business that was well worth having, or paid someone to do a job of any size or significance, he would, at the right time, make you a present by way of kum-shaw. To the Chinese it must have been obvious that the proper time for giving kum-shaw to Europeans was Christmas, this being the season when they gave presents to each other. Thus, I presume, the phenomenon of Christmas kum-shaw came about.

The origin of the custom is a bit speculative, but it does at least explain that if you dealt regularly with the same grocer, he would make you a present of some free groceries at Christmas. I first became aware of the practice when two coolies came trotting into the office with a long bamboo pole between them, with three cases of whisky hanging off it. One was for Trevor Knight, one for Jock Campbell and one for me, being Christmas kum-shaw from the stevedores who loaded and unloaded the ships. I thought this was very kind of them, particularly as I had done absolutely nothing to deserve it. I had not appointed them, I had no power to fire them, I was not required to keep an eye on them, and all I ever did was exchange a few friendly words with a head stevedore who used to come into the office from time to time.

This generosity of the stevedores was a quiet and discreet affair compared to the behaviour of the hawkers. Clearly I had become a figure of terror to the hawking community, every one of whom must have been convinced that I had to be placated with Christmas kum-shaw to stop me from cancelling their boarding passes. It started when one of the nice old ladies came and tried to present me with a Swatow lace tablecloth. This alarmed me very much, as I did not want to accept any present from her, or to deplete her stock, and furthermore had no great use for a tablecloth. However, she became very distressed when I tried to get out of taking it, so I went and consulted Trevor Knight, my boss, and he said that this was the custom of the country. I should take the tablecloth, as otherwise she would be very worried and wonder what she had done wrong. The rule, he said, was that I might accept anything but money, so I took the tablecloth and thanked the lady, after which the floodgates opened. I was showered with silk shirts, which I do not like, tailors found the way to the flat where I lived and arrived with tape measures in their hands, pleading with me to stand still to be measured for a suit. A self-winding Bulova watch was pressed upon me, although I had a much better Longines which I was perfectly capable of winding. I forget whatever else I got, but it seemed so close to accepting bribes that I was very uncomfortable about the whole affair, and greatly relieved when Christmas was over and the flow of kum-shaw dried up.

Mercifully, it only happened once. By the next Christmas I had been posted to Japan, where none of this went on.

Chapter 8

Hong Kong – Water Sports

In those days, and perhaps still today, people in Hong Kong tended to be classified by the name of their employer, rather as American slaves were known by the name of their owner. They said things like, "Do you know Bill Smith? – He's Hong Kong Bank" or, "Have you met Tom Brown? - He's Jardine Matheson." It seemed odd, at first, to be introduced to a walking bank or an ambulant shipping line, but one got used to it.

There was a fairly strict hierarchical structure throughout the business community. The man at the top of a firm was usually called the Taipan, which must be the Chinese for the Man at the Top, but sometimes he was called the Number One. "He's the Bank Line Number One," they said, rather than Chief Executive, Managing Director or anything like that. The Swire Group still very kindly send me their newsletter and it now bristles with details of people with impressive titles such as General Manager, Technical Services and Sustainability, or IM Head, Corporate and Back-Office Operations. There was none of that in my day. People either just had names, like Mr Mok Hing Kong, or titles you could understand, like Blue Funnel Agent.

Within the hierarchy I was, of course at the bottom of the heap, about as far from being Number One as it was possible to get – probably Number Eight, or something like that. All the same, the people higher up were very friendly and often used to invite me to lunch or dinner. These were usually pleasant occasions, but their hospitality often extended to asking me to go sailing, and that was not so pleasant.

Hong Kong, being an island, is a great place for sailing, and the two principal sports in my time were sailing and golf. The golf course was on the mainland in a countrified area among rice fields with a road running through the middle, and beside the road was a mildly ominous and not very helpful notice with the words, "Beware of Flying Golf Balls." There was a cricket club in the centre of things, very close to the Butterfields office, which I joined as it was a good place to have lunch, but I had no wish to play cricket and had never played golf. Sailing, though, was a different matter.

It was axiomatic among the people of the colony that sailing was a thoroughly delightful pastime. The Royal Hong Kong Yacht Club was a most thriving institution, and I expect that in the letter that came to me from the Oxford University Appointments Board, the pleasures of sailing figured among the advantages of working in Hong Kong. I had never been sailing, but I had read the Swallows and Amazons novels, and from these, with my general observation of the way sailing people talked, it did not occur to me to doubt that sailing was an absolutely capital affair.

It took me some time to come to a firm conclusion, and I had to piece things together gradually before I got a picture of the whole. I did not understand at first the personality change which can come over a man at the helm of a boat. As I was about Number Eight in the office, naturally those senior to me had to tell me what to do, which in working hours they always did in a calm and helpful manner. Once they got in a boat, though, they started to snap out orders in a way that was not always agreeable, and if these orders were not carried out to their liking, they lost their tempers.

Tempers are very often lost in boats, and I can tell you exactly why. It is because a great many things can go wrong, such as the boat capsizing or the boom breaking or a rope fouling the propeller (if there is one, which there usually was). This perpetual risk means that the man in charge is generally on edge, and people who are on edge lose their tempers very easily.

Breaking the boom seemed to be an ever-present danger, but I only knew one man who actually contrived to do it. I wasn't there at the time, but he managed it by standing on the boom and diving off it into the sea. He was quite a fat chap, and his weight simply broke the thing in two. After that the boat was helplessly drifting towards the coast of communist China, and had it reached the shore he would have probably been locked up as a spy, but somehow he managed to get a message to the coastguard, who kindly rescued him.

A more conventional way to break the boom is to get in a muddle when changing direction. The first step in this process is for the helmsman to shout out, "ready about!" which I always thought to be a foolish sort of remark. To a man fresh from National Service in the army, turning about meant turning through 180^0, but in a boat it seemed to mean aiming the bow off to the left rather than to the right or to the right rather than the left depending on the way it was pointing at the time. Anyway, having shouted "ready about" the helmsman, after a short pause, always shouted "Lee-o" which certainly struck me as a thoroughly silly thing to say. Military commands, such as "quick march" or "eyes right" were always meaningful, but as well as sounding silly "Lee-o" had no obvious meaning at all.

Be that as it may, when the helmsman shouted "Lee-o" the proper thing for the crew, which in this case might well be me, was *either* to pull on what they called the sheets and to let go what were known as the runners, or, contrary wise, to let go the sheets and pull on the runners. It was of the utmost importance to get this right, as to pull on the sheets when you should be letting them go, or to let go the runners when you should be pulling on them, was one of the ways in which you could, under the right circumstances, break the boom or capsize the boat.

The difficulty from my point of view was that both sheets and runners were virtually identical bits of rope and I could not tell one from the other. This being so the chances of my getting it wrong were exactly even, and I was just as likely to pull and let go the wrong ones as the right ones, which frequently caused the man in charge to lose his temper and start shouting. The wholly ridiculous thing was that the two bits of rope could perfectly easily have been colour coded. If they had bound the ends of the sheets with green string and the ends of the runners with red then instead of "Lee-o" they could have said "Let go green!" whereupon I would have let go the sheets with unerring accuracy, and would have pulled on the runners without being told. I can see no reason against this, but I suppose that they had simply never thought of anything so simple.

Ignoring these technicalities, I found that the pleasures of sailing, even when in the most competent hands, are at best questionable. Once, and only once, I felt that I had got the hang of what was supposed to be the attraction. The wind was blowing fiercely, the boat was charging into the waves and bucking like a horse, spray was flying everywhere and water was washing all over the deck. "This is more like it," I said to the man at the helm.

"It's getting dangerous" he replied. "We had better go back."

The opposite extreme, which is much more common, is that the boat wallows up and down in the same place, or else advances painfully slowly if there happens to be a gentle breeze. In this case there is nothing to do but look at the sea which is not at all interesting, or the shore, which may be very pretty but either remains the same however long you look at it, or else changes so slowly that the change is virtually imperceptible.

The conclusion at which I arrived after some weeks was that sailing is generally either dull or dangerous, and that the bit in between is so rarely achieved that it is not worth the trouble and anxiety involved, to say nothing of the possible expense and/or discomfort. This neat appraisal did not dawn upon me by degrees, but arrived as a revelation. I was lying in bed musing upon my life and I thought to myself, "There's something about this place that I do not like. I feel this to be so but I am not sure what it is." And then I thought some more, and it came to me: "It is *sailing*. All that ready-abouting and lee-oing - I just don't like it. I shan't do it anymore." Having reached this comfortable conclusion I went peacefully to sleep.

After that, when asked to go sailing I used to decline as politely as possible, explaining that it was something that I did not really enjoy. This was thought to be very eccentric by nearly everyone except my boss Trevor Knight, who, as a cricket and golf man, thought I was quite sensible.

All this is true of yachts both large and small. The larger ones in Hong Kong had small cramped cabins in which you could sleep if you wanted, and in this respect they were much like caravans. One might adapt Dr Johnson's famous comparison of a ship and a prison, and say that being in a yacht is like being in a caravan with the chance of being drowned.

*

Having disposed of sailing in its immediate effect on my life in 1954, I will add that it can give grounds for divorce. Generally speaking, it is men who like sailing and women who don't. In the early stages of a romance the woman will persuade herself that she too finds sailing enjoyable and will join in with every appearance of enthusiasm. Then as the years pass and ardour cools, she will come to face the fact that she hates the discomfort and the smell and the boredom and the bad temper, and would rather have nothing to do with it. On this point the marriage may founder. If she declares she will sail no more, her husband may be left without a crew, and there is a real danger that if he has to choose between his wife and his boat, he will choose the boat. I knew a man who divorced two wives in succession on these grounds, and then took a third who was much younger than himself. Whether from having too young a wife or from doing too much sailing, he died while she was still at the enthusiastic stage, and so saved himself the trouble of looking out for a fourth. As a foundation for a happy marriage, sailing is decidedly risky.

It is a pity that sailing did not appeal to me, as I am no good at ball games, which put cricket and golf out of the question. However I needed some sort of exercise and one of the things I could do to a reasonable standard was to row in a boat although I am really too small and light for an oarsman. Hong Kong had a Victoria Rowing Club, so I joined and turned up from time to time for an outing in a scratch pair or four. Bouncing about in the sea was a different matter from rowing on the smooth water of the Isis at Oxford, and I did not greatly care for it, but I took part in a regatta in which I stroked a four to victory and won a silver jam spoon. This was one of the two sporting trophies that I have won in my life, the other being the minute silver cup which I got for winning the under-ten 100 yards at my preparatory school. In spite of my little triumph as a Hong Kong oarsman, I gave up the water in favour of the greater attractions of the Jockey Club.

Chapter 9

Hong Kong – The Jockey Club

In 1954 racing at the Hong Kong Jockey Club was not the superior affair that it is now, with world-class horses and world-famous jockeys competing at one or other of its two racecourses. There was one racecourse, all the riders were amateurs, and they raced on ponies about the size of polo ponies.

My credentials as a horseman were neither very good nor very bad. Under the tutelage of the Prussian Count who was riding master to the Eighth Hussars, I progressed to the point that I rode in four Rhine Army races. I was left at the start in a flat race; my horse jumped the wings in a steeplechase; the animal I rode in a hurdle race ran out of steam halfway round, but I finished a respectable fourth in a point-to-point. I thought this ought to be good enough to allow me at least to ride exercise in Hong Kong, and possibly to ride in the races.

There was no help to be got from Butterfields. No one else in the firm was even a member of the Jockey Club, let alone interested in riding. Also there was a rule that no one working for Butterfields might ride in the races without permission of the Taipan. When I say there was a rule, I mean that people told me there was such a rule. There was no rule book in which the rules could be looked up, but it was most devoutly believed by one and all that such a rule existed. It was, they said, the fault of some past Chief Accountant who was a heavy gambler and had lost a lot of the firm's money on the ponies. Accordingly I wrote to the Taipain respectfully asking permission to join the Jockey Club and ride, to which he agreed without demur but with some surprise, as he seemed to be the only person who had never heard of the rule.

There were three more obstacles to be got over. I had to become a member of the Jockey Club, for which there was a waiting list; I had to find a trainer to give me rides and, I had to find a way to get to the racecourse at the right time.

They were all solved quite easily. Being, as I have said, a sort of Butterfields Number Eight, I met another Number Eight in a different firm of which his father was not only Number One but also a Steward of the Jockey Club and owner of several ponies. This Number Eight introduced me to the paternal Number One and I filled in a form and the Number One took it and the next thing, I was in. He further most kindly said that he would introduce me to his trainer, who would see what could be done by way of rides. To take advantage of this I needed to be at the racecourse very early. As all riders were amateurs it was assumed that they all had offices to go to, which was certainly true in my case, as I had to be at my desk by 9am. In order to fit everything in, they started riding before dawn, and to get any rides I certainly needed to be on the spot by 6am, and 5.30 would be better.

The Butterfields Duty Mess was about 2½ miles from the racecourse in Happy Valley. To reach it from the office I took the cable car to the top of the Peak and walked along a footpath from which there was a wonderful view and a constant noise, unique to Hong Kong, made by the feet of hundreds of coolies in wooden-soled sandals trotting along the roads below, mingled with the clattering and clanging of trams.

For purposes of reaching Happy Valley the cable car was no good as it did not run at 5.30am and anyway the stop at the bottom was a long way from the racecourse, so I bought a bicycle. This was thought to be odd, and was certainly unique. In all my time in Hong Kong I never met, saw or heard of another European on a bicycle, but it answered admirably. I could zoom down the Peak on the empty roads in the dark, speed to the Jockey Club and later ride easily back to my office. I only rode the bicycle downhill or on the flat. The coolie boy employed at the mess used to come down into town to do the shopping, so I got him to take the bicycle back on the cable car when he had finished. In the mysterious way of the Chinese, I believe he gained a certain amount of face from being allowed to cross the threshold of the Butterfields building, and from being entrusted with the important task of looking after my bicycle, which I graciously permitted him to ride.

The Stewards of the Hong Kong Jockey Club did not just allow any new arrival to get on a pony and mingle with the other riders without making sure that he was reasonably competent. Accordingly it was arranged that I should ride under the eyes of the assembled Stewards on a pony called Ben Lawers. Ben Lawers came with an evil reputation, having broken the collarbone of another rider not long before. His trick, I was told, was to go along freely, then stop dead, dig in his toes and hope to shoot his rider over his head. I was told to trot him round the cinder track on which the exercising was done, and he gave me no trouble, though we did get shouted at rather a lot. It was a rule that ponies were to be trotted while it was still dark, and once it got light, trotting was to stop and galloping to begin. As the Stewards wanted to watch me I had to ride in the light, and as they told me to trot, trot I did, and so got shouted at for trotting in galloping time. It was a surprise, as I didn't know what I was doing wrong, but anyway I was passed fit to ride exercise and so, six mornings a week, I got myself to Happy Valley by half past five in the morning.

It was all very interesting and rather odd. There were two paddocks, the Russian paddock and the Chinese paddock. Every morning those ponies trained by Chinese trainers were gathered in one paddock and those trained by Russian trainers in the other. There were no other trainers – just Chinese and Russians. I was told, though I cannot vouch for it, that the Russians were from a Cossack regiment which had mutinied in 1917, seized a ship in Vladivostok, and sailed it to Hong Kong to escape the revolution. Knowing nothing much about anything except soldiering and horses, some of them set up as trainers and had acquired the right to train about half the ponies.

European owners tended to patronise the Russian trainers, and Chinese owners the Chinese. The trainer for whom I rode was called Leskoff, sometimes known as Pop, a little wizened Russian who was normally quite genial but could fly into terrible rages in a Russian sort of way. I remember him snatching his cap off his head and jumping up and down on it in a fury, at something that someone – luckily not me – had done, which is the sort of thing I feel a man might do in a play by Chekov. As applied to Pop, the Cossack theory was quite credible. Had he been, say, 25 years old in 1917 he would have been 62 in 1954 and I should think he was older than that.

The ponies had numbers as well as names, and Pop never knew their names, only their numbers. He issued his orders in White Russian English, saying things like, "You ride 27 twice round trotting." At this a pony with 27 on its saddlecloth would loom up out of the dark, led by a groom who gave me a leg up, took us onto the track and let go. To start with I had no idea what pony I was on apart from its number, but after a bit I got to know their names and personalities. I remember one called Hiram C, who was very furry and used to growl like a dog – "This very pulling pony you be careful," was Pop's instruction the first time I rode him. There was one called Hellzapoppin who bolted with me, which luckily Pop thought was hilarious. There was a mare I didn't much like because when the groom let go, she wouldn't go forwards or backwards, just spun round in circles cannoning off other riders until she suddenly changed her mind, snatched the bit between her teeth and charged forward into the darkness.

In time I was promoted to galloping as well as trotting. Pop would say, "You go half mile last quarter 28" which meant that I was to gallop for half a mile and do the last quarter mile in 28 seconds. You might think it difficult to judge your speed to the second, but curiously enough it was quite easy, and I never remember Pop complaining that I had gone too fast or too slowly. Then, after some weeks I was given a ride in a novice race and so became one of a small band who gave regular amusement to thousands of people and caused huge sums of money to change hands.

Although we were all amateur riders, you are not to think of the Hong Kong Jockey Club as a tin-pot little affair, as if it were a glorified adult version of the Pony Club. On the contrary, it was a magnificent undertaking. There was a huge stand with luxurious boxes for the owners, there were palatial stables for the ponies and, it was said, the Jockey Club made a bigger profit than the Hong Kong Bank. All of this came from the Chinese passion for gambling.

The silliest gambling I ever came across was on a trip to the Portuguese enclave of Macao, where a lot of obviously rich Chinese were playing *fan tan* in the casino. To play *fan tan* you need a bucket of trouser buttons, a scoop, a paper-knife and a table. The croupier scoops up a quantity of buttons from the bucket and spills them onto the table in a heap. At this point bets are placed, after which the croupier takes his paper-knife and divides the heap into two piles. Next, with his knife, he moves four buttons away from the left pile, and then four buttons from the right pile, and keeps going like that until at the end he is left with 3, 2, 1 or no buttons. It is on this outcome that the punters have placed their bets – on whether the number of buttons in the scoop was exactly divisible by four, or whether there would be a remainder of 1, 2 or 3. To people who could be totally absorbed, as they seemed to be, in something so ridiculous, the more sophisticated pastime of betting on ponies had great appeal.

There was no casino in Hong Kong and, apart from a Sweep run by the government, the Jockey Club had cleverly cornered the gambling market. There were no bookmakers either on or off the course, and all bets were processed through the Tote in Happy Valley. From all the money bet by all the punters on every race, the government took 5% and the Jockey Club kept 10%, after which the rest was paid out in winnings. Such was the local enthusiasm for this arrangement that, after the club had met all its expenses the Stewards were left with a handsome surplus with which they did good works. If you remember Mr Blair, one time Prime Minister, you may recall that he was very keen on "schools n' hospitals" and the Stewards of the Hong Kong Jockey Club were there before him. There was, and is, a most impressive list of schools and hospitals, and also sports facilities, endowed by the Jockey Club for the benefit of the Chinese community.

In playing my part in this charitable undertaking I was at the base of a sort of pyramid. At the top were three riders, one French, one Chinese and one English, each of whom had been champion jockey at least once in the past. They were sure of a ride in every race except those confined to novices. Below them was a band of some ten or twelve who had ridden at least ten winners and so were no longer novices, and they rode pretty regularly in the open races. Most of them were Chinese, but I can remember one Australian, one Portuguese and one Indian among them. Then, at the base of the pyramid were all of us novices who gratefully took whatever rides we were given. We numbered about twenty five. One of us was French, one was of unknown nationality but had the unusual name of H Fattydad, and all the rest, myself excepted, were Chinese.

Being a member of this fraternity had several effects on my social life, one of which was that I started falling asleep at dinner parties. Hard drinking and late hours were normal, on top of which there were two damnable developments by way of entertainment. England was still shaking off the years of wartime austerity, but Hong Kong had everything, and at one time expensive cameras and colour slides were the latest thing, which then gave way to cine cameras and black and white film. In either case, after dinner the host was likely to put up a screen, draw the curtains and start showing his beastly slides or his boring film. For a man who had been up since 5 that morning, ridden three or four ponies and done a day's work, to start drinking at 8pm and not eat till after 9 made it hard enough to stay awake anyway, but in a blacked-out room it was impossible. Everyone else was oo-ing and ah-ing while I slumbered through the whole thing. When they put the lights on I had to shake myself awake and say how frightfully good and interesting it had been, hoping that no one had noticed that I had missed the entire show.

My racing career can be dealt with briefly. We have a little cine film which shows Deirdre, who is now my wife and was then my fiancée, leading me in to unsaddle after a race, and my grandson is convinced that we were on the way to the winner's enclosure, but I fear that I was only second. The sorry truth is that, though I landed tremendous odds by being placed on a pony called Cornhill who was thought to have no chance whatever, and though from time to time I was second or third in other races, I never rode an outright winner in either of the two seasons in which I was riding. No doubt this was due to my incompetent horsemanship, but also perhaps because I did not take enough risks as I was quite keen not to break my neck.

It was a dangerous pastime in its way. I suppose we galloped at about 35 miles an hour, and the course was small with fairly sharp turns, so that if there was any kind of a crash it could be a bad one. I have read that one year there were nine accidents in one season, which persuaded the Chinese community that there must be vengeful ghosts at work so Buddhist priests were brought in to perform the necessary rites to pacify them. In spite of this, the great Marcel Samarcq, twice champion jockey, was killed outright the following year, which made further ceremonies necessary. These lasted for three days and four nights and involved forty-nine monks who, said the South China Morning Post, "paraded in grave progression around the track, praying Buddha to purify it."

Whatever the reason for my mediocre showing, I must have made my mark somehow. Many years later my daughter went to Hong Kong and was taken on a visit to the stables. There she was introduced to a trainer called Alex Lam, and being told that he had been a jockey in the old days, she said, "Perhaps you knew my father, Edward Enfield?"

"Mr Enfield!" he exclaimed "The last of the amateur jockeys!"

His memory deceived him as there were others after me, but if I had carried on for some years longer and then fallen victim to the vengeful ghosts, that would have made an admirable inscription on my tombstone.

I have hinted that the Jockey Club had several effects on my social life, a topic which is best dealt with in a separate chapter.

Chapter 10

Hong Kong Life

Life in Hong Kong was both stratified and segregated. By stratified I mean that as a Number Eight in Butterfields my acquaintance could easily have been limited to Number Eights in other firms plus Number Eights, and those above me but not too far above me, in Butterfields itself. By segregated I mean that there were clubs to which Chinese were not admitted, beaches where Chinese were not allowed, and that the two races tended to keep apart socially. Apart from my enforced service in the Hong Kong Defence Force, to which I will come in a moment, I might have spent all my time in the colony without having anything much to do with anyone Chinese except in office hours. Luckily for me it turned out otherwise.

There were some places where the colour bar, if it can be called that, had no effect. There was no distinction among the races in the lower ranks of the Defence Force; the bar did not apply among lawyers as there were both Chinese and European magistrates, barristers and solicitors who all mingled socially in a sensible manner; it did not apply at Government House because the governor, as part of his duties, regularly entertained rich Chinese merchants, of whom there were many. There was no distinction amongst the riders at the Jockey Club, who were a cosmopolitan collection with a Chinese majority. My life was greatly improved by all of these. I rather enjoyed being a private in the Defence Force, I had a good friend among the lawyers, I dined once at Government House and my fellow jockeys were a most friendly lot altogether. Also there was Mabel, but I will come to her later.

To take the Defence Force first, this was something like the Territorial Army in England. I forget the age range but all young and able bodied holders of British passports were required to join, and we were to act with the regular forces to drive off the invading hordes of Mao Tse Tung if he chose to send his armies across the border. No account was taken of previous service or experience, so they made me a private, issued me with boots and a uniform, and set about teaching me how to turn to the right, turn to the left, and other things that I had done for two years in my National Service. I had to go to a drill hall to be taught these unnecessary lessons by a drill sergeant who was on secondment from the regular army, which he clearly regarded as a cushy number.

Most of us privates were Chinese. There was a special kind of Hong Kong British passport which conferred some particular status but did not, when the colony came to an end, include the right to come to live in Britain. Whatever the advantages may have been, one of the requirements was service in the Defence Force, and when they called the roll it went something like this:

"Aw, Boon Mok" – "Sir!"

"Bao, Lai Wen" – "Sir!"

"Chan, Jee Ling" – "Sir!"

"Enfield" – "Sir!"

"Fok, Ah Lui" – "Sir!"

"King, Tse Woo" – "Sir!" – and so on with perhaps an occasional Remedios or da Silva when they reached someone of Portuguese origin.

As well as drills in the drill hall we went on occasional weekend exercises on the mainland and, once a year, a fortnightly camp. I had some difficulty in stopping my fellow soldiers from treating me as if I were one of Kipling's British soldiers and they were to behave like a lot of Chinese Gunga Dins. I managed to cling onto my rifle and pack, which they wanted to carry for me, and on night exercises I did not let them help me across the paddy fields in the dark, but I gladly let them do the cooking. Usually we were fed out of a field kitchen, but sometimes we were given rice which we were left to cook in government-issue mess tins over impromptu campfires. They all were brilliant cooks under these conditions, which I wasn't, so I gratefully accepted their help.

I liked the rank of private soldier. Military equipment nowadays is much more sophisticated than it was in my time, and present day soldiers are far more highly skilled and trained than they were in 1954. In my day infantrymen had rifles but nothing much more in the way of weapons, and to be a private in the Hong Kong Defence Force was much like being a duck in a line of ducks, waddling along in accordance with orders. If they told us to advance, we advanced; if they said stop, we stopped; if they said lie down we lay down. It was all extremely easy and restful, made even more enjoyable by the sight of officers running up and down with maps, trying to make out where they were or what they were meant to be doing.

Where I came out strong, though I say it myself, was as a wireless operator. Infantrymen in those days did not much like using the wireless, and preferred shouting, blowing whistles, and waving their arms, but they had portable wirelesses called 88 sets which did not work very well and which they tried not to use. I, on the other hand, had done my National Service in a tank, and tanks communicate by wireless all the time as there is no other way to do it, so by infantry standards I was an outright wizard at wireless procedure. Once my extraordinary talents were discovered I was made company signaller and attached to company HQ, in which capacity I distinguished myself by devising an entirely new method of teaching wireless procedure.

The idea came to me as we were trudging along on a route march with nothing much to think about, so I livened things up with a game of Twenty Questions played on the 88 sets.

In case you are not familiar with the game, in ordinary Twenty Questions the question master thinks of an object and tells the players that it is either Animal, Vegetable or Mineral, but he doesn't tell them anything else. They then ask him questions to which he must answer either yes or no, but nothing more. If they get to the right answer in twenty questions or less, they have won.

As played on the 88 set it is called, in the military language of the time, Figures Two Zero Questions, because "Figures Two Zero" was how you were supposed to say "Twenty" on air. I, being Control, was question master, and the signallers of the three other platoons were callsigns One, Two and Three. The game played according to wireless procedure of the time went like this:

Control: "Hello all stations, we will now play Figures Two Zero Questions. The first object is Vegetable. Out."

One: "Hello One – can you eat it? Over."

Control: "One. No, you cannot eat it. Figures one question. Out."

Two: "Hello Two – can you wear it? Over."

Control: "Two – No, you cannot wear it. Figures two questions. Out."

So it proceeds, and as they get closer to the answer the game becomes more exciting, and then they forget proper procedure. Callsign Three may jam Callsign Two by coming in when Two is still sending, at which Control may say: "Hello Two. Hello Three. Three – do not jam. Out to you. Two, say again all after flagpole – over."

Two: "Two. Has the flagpole got one on it? Over."

Control: "Two, your correct transmission would be: 'I say again, has the flagpole got figures one on it?' The answer is yes – it has got figures one on it. Figures one – seven questions. Out."

This is such a good way of practising wireless procedure that I felt I should write to the Adjutant at Sandhurst to tell him of this remarkable advance in the training of signallers, but I never got round to it. Perhaps I will send him a copy of this book.

My friend in legal circles was Oswald Cheung who had been at Oxford with me and was now a successful barrister at the Hong Kong bar. He was older than me, having seen war service in China, and took me under his wing when I looked him up. He had a country house where he gave parties for all nationalities and he had a yacht. Sailing with Ossie was at least tolerable as he had a boat boy who did all the work. Ossie told the boy where to go and we sat in the bows and drank gin and tonic. Once there, we swam while the boat boy cooked lunch. On one such outing as I climbed back on board I saw the triangular fin of a shark rise above the water and disappear just where I had been swimming. I had heard a few explosions and hadn't taken any notice but I now saw there was a fisherman throwing dynamite into the water, which stuns the fish and makes them easy to scoop up. The shark had come in for some easy pickings and as people did occasionally get taken by sharks in Hong Kong, I suppose he might have eaten me if he was still hungry and I had been in his path.

As well as taking me swimming in shark-infested waters, Ossie, who was then still a bachelor, showed me something of the town. One evening we ended up in a fairly low class nightclub called the Hung Lau, which means Red Room, in the seedier part of Hong Kong, which is called Wanchai. What you did in the Hung Lau was drink expensive drinks and dance with taxi dancers, these being Chinese girls who sidled up and sat down at your table and said hello. I don't think we paid them for their company but they drank tonic water and we were charged for gin and tonic. The one who sidled up to me was very pretty and said her name was Looby. She was bright and good fun so I had an enjoyable evening with Looby, in spite of my being a lousy dancer. Then as we went home (without Looby or any other girl, in case you were wondering) Ossie thought it necessary to warn me that, whatever arrangements I might come to in the future, if I were asked to a party and told that I might bring a girl, I should under no circumstances whatever bring Looby. This I tell you because, the way things were, there was no possibility of my going out with a respectable Chinese girl, as everyone would have taken her for a Looby, and caused her great embarrassment. Which brings me to Mabel.

As I think back to the Mabel episode, it seems to me altogether remarkable. It came about because a senior person in Butterfields gave me two documents and told me to go to the dockyard. There I would meet a Chinese lady whom I should ask to sign both documents. One of these she was to keep and the other I was to bring back. The effect would be to transfer a tug from the ownership of Butterfields to the ownership of a Mr Danton Kwok, the Chinese lady being, I understood, his assistant.

So I went, and she came, and she signed the papers, and we chatted. Her name, I discovered, was Mabel. She was older than me, but by no means so old as to be out of reach. She was attractive and I have no doubt was wearing a cheong saam, a Chinese dress which has gone out of fashion, but in Hong Kong at the time was almost universal. It is a silk sheath dress split at the side up to the thighs, which looks ridiculous on Europeans but very becoming on tall slender Chinese ladies such as Mabel. How I guessed that she might possibly be willing to let me take her out, I cannot think. How I dared to ask for her phone number, I cannot conceive. Why she consented to give it to me, I cannot explain, but she did, so one day I rang her up and we met, and carried on from there.

She was divorced, so I was not causing any danger to a marriage, but otherwise it was against all the rules. In the Hong Kong of 1955 the young men of Butterfields were not supposed to be going out with Chinese divorcees and respectable Chinese divorcees were not supposed to be seen in the company of young men from Butterfields. I cannot say that we ignored this aspect of affairs altogether but we didn't bother much about it. By this I mean that we met and went around quite openly. In the hot weather Chinese ladies, including Mabel, often wore thin cotton pyjamas as an alternative to the cheong saam, and I remember thinking it odd to be going to the cinema with a Chinese lady in pyjamas. It is not something I ever expected. On the other hand I was just a little discreet. I did not mention Mabel to Ossie Cheung or tell my flatmates about her, but I used from time to time to disappear without saying where I was going.

Mabel was a bit more open. She introduced me to Mr Danton Kwok and we went on a launch picnic on his big and ostentatious yacht. Danton Kwok, she told me, had been a smuggler and got very rich but was now reformed and going into property.

"What did he smuggle?"

"Steel, mostly," was the answer.

At that time there was an embargo on selling certain strategic items to China and there was a lot of money to be made by running the customs blockade and dealing in such things as steel. It struck me that the tug which led to our meeting was not likely to be of much use to a property developer but might well come in handy for a smuggler, so perhaps he wasn't altogether reformed. It would, however, have been indiscreet to put this point to Mr Kwok and anyway it was impossible, as he spoke no word of English.

I suppose I wondered vaguely what would happen if this little liaison came to light, and the answer, more or less, was nothing. Eventually someone saw us together after which I came in for a bit of envious teasing by some, and jealous disapproval from others, but beyond that, nothing. We carried on in the same way until, after some months, it came to an end, as such things do. We did not quarrel, we just parted, a little sadly perhaps, but inevitably.

*

I have said that I dined once at Government House, and this was not my doing but my father's. He came on a visit to Hong Kong and as he had been a senior civil servant some message was passed to Government House from the Colonial Office in London. We went and signed the visitors' book and were invited to dinner. It was a marvellously regimented affair. We dressed in our dinner jackets. We were told that a car would come for us at 7.15 and at 7.15 precisely a limousine appeared. We were swept through the gates of Government House and seized upon by an ADC in police dress uniform, who briefed us. My father was to take a visiting dowager countess into dinner and to sit near to the governor; I was to trail along in the rear and sit at the end of the table by the ADC. We were presented to the governor, given drinks and allowed to mingle with the other guests, with the ADC making introductions.

After half an hour the governor led the way into dinner. My only recollection of the conversation was that the ADC, who was a young man of my own age or less, opened the batting by saying, "Tell me, Mr Enfield, sir – how do you spend your spare time?" From where I sat I could see that the governor was conversing affably with my father, the countess, and various prosperous-looking Chinese who were within speaking distance. At a quarter to ten the governor rose to his feet and we all rose to ours. He led the way out and we followed, then he stood by the door – we filed past, made our goodbyes, and were swept away in the limousine. I think we were back at my father's hotel by 10 o'clock. The governor must have been the only man in Hong Kong who kept early hours.

As well as an introduction to Government House, my father had a letter to a Chinese magistrate called Hin Shing Lo, whose daughter he had met in London. The Lo family were the only Chinese I came across who put their names in the European order, as the daughter was Helen Lo and the magistrate was known to his friends as Hin Shing. He was the most friendly of men, and took my father and me to a Chinese restaurant where there was a band and a dance floor. So that we should not be short of company he brought his wife and two of his concubines. (I was told that there were more at home.) Much to my surprise, and much to his, my elderly father, a former pillar of the Ministry of Agriculture and Fisheries, found himself shuffling round the dance floor with his arms clasped round a Chinese concubine.

Hin Shing Lo also figured in Deirdre's life, and it is time that she was properly introduced. She was working for what was called the Security Liaison Office, which passed itself off as being a branch of the War Office. Either because I am short of curiosity, or because she put a stop to any discussions, I never really asked what this office was for, or what she did. The only thing I knew was that when ships' captains arrived with a cargo from Shanghai or Tientsien, they used to go and report to the Security Liaison Office, so I supposed that the War Office were curious to know if they had happened to notice any battleships or submarines while they were there. Years afterwards I asked her was it anything to do with MI5 and she thought I was remarkably stupid not to have worked out that it was exactly that.

My children like to tell their offspring that their granny was a spy but it is not true. The newspapers of today cannot tell the difference between MI6, who are spies, and MI5, who are counter-spies, so they lump them together and call them all spies. When, in the course of time, Deirdre and I became engaged, she had to submit my details to higher authority in case she had become a security risk by taking up with me. I suppose that should have roused my curiosity, but anyway they took no exception to me, which I feel was a failure on their part. If they had looked into my background properly they would have found that my father's sister Elinor was married to a full-time top-notch communist called Emil Burns. I am sure they must have had a fat file on Emil Burns back in London, as he was an eminent communist and one-time editor of the Daily Worker, so Deirdre should have been instantly dismissed.

I may say that Emil Burns was a very nice uncle-in-law, in spite of his communist sympathies. Both he and my aunt Elinor were very intelligent but slightly mad. I don't know Emil's background but Elinor had read English at Oxford. They had, not surprisingly, absolutely no interest in football until Moscow Dynamo came on the scene and started beating a number of English sides. After that both Elinor and Emil solemnly lectured my unhappy father on the superior teamwork, remarkable footwork and outstanding ball control of players brought up under the communist system.

*

Deirdre and I met when she came to tea at the Duty Mess, which I was sharing with two other fellows, one of whom was called Gus. She came with Marianne, with whom she was sharing a flat, they both being acquainted with Gus. Deirdre told me later that as they left Marianne said to her, about me, "He's like a lizard, isn't he?" To which Deirdre replied "Yes." I have puzzled over this for years. Why a lizard? I do not move from place to place in sudden darts. I can see no facial resemblance. Did I give them the impression that I might at any moment gobble one of them up with a flick of my tongue? Whatever the explanation she must have found my lizard-like qualities to be at least bearable, which was

94

lucky for me, as life took a great turn for the better when we started going out.

I have to explain that Deirdre is one of those who, at a party, will manage to speak to everybody before she goes home. Also, she was very pretty and attractive, and so she fitted in everywhere. She was just the person to come to dinner parties and cover for me if I fell asleep. She got on famously with Ossie Cheung and willingly joined in his sort of sailing. She loyally accompanied me on a launch picnic laid on by a firm of Chinese stevedores, and she was a huge hit at the Jockey Club.

We went to the races regularly. The stewards gave me a Riders badge plus another badge for a guest which allowed us to go to the Riders and Owners box rather than jostling with the crowds below. Also, if I was riding for an owner who had a private box I was always, most kindly, invited to lunch beforehand, and once Deirdre had been spotted they asked her as well. Looking back I can say that I do not recall coming across any other young, pretty, socially adept English girl in the Owners and Riders box or in one of the private boxes, so she was a rarity and a huge success, particularly with the Taipans and Number Ones who were the sort of people to have private boxes.

She also went down very well with my father when he came on his visit. They swapped stories about Hin Shing Lo, the magistrate. Deirdre had appeared in his court as a witness because she had woken one morning to find a strange man in her bedroom. She shouted at him to go away, and he left, but this was not the end of the matter. The cook-amah who looked after Deirdre and Marianne, name of Ah Luk, had seen him and said that she would know him again. Accordingly the police were told, a few likely suspects rounded up, and Ah Luk and Deirdre picked him out at an identity parade. In court he pleaded guilty to whatever the charge may have been, and in mitigation his counsel assured the court that he had not meant any harm but just liked climbing into girls' bedrooms for a bit of excitement, "like a small boy climbing into an orchard to steal apples." At this Hin Ching Lo turned, gazed at Deirdre over the top of his spectacles, and remarked, "In this case, the apples do not appear to have been stolen."

*

I remember exactly the day when I thought of asking her to marry me, which was 14th February 1955. The Jockey Club had a country establishment on the mainland where you could, among other things, ride out among the hills and rice fields on retired race ponies. We were doing that when Deirdre came off her pony, hit her head and knocked herself slightly silly. She was not seriously concussed but she was confused, particularly about the date. As we rode quietly back to the stables she kept asking me what day it was to which, for the sake of variety, I gave different answers. Sometimes I said Sunday, sometimes the 14th of February and sometimes Sunday the 14th of February and then I took to saying, "St Valentine's Day – the 14th of February" or "Sunday – St Valentine's Day". Now when you have told a girl over and over again that it is St Valentine's Day it does strike you that you ought perhaps to do something about it, such as ask her to marry you. I didn't do it then, though, but thought about it for some weeks, and as it still seemed a good idea, I proposed and was accepted.

This brought us up against another Butterfield rule. The original document which came from the Oxford Appointments Board had said that Swire employees were not allowed to marry unless they were at least 30 years old and had put in 7 years of service. I did not give this a moment's thought when I joined, as at that time marriage to me was rather like death, which I regarded as something which happened to other people. Now I was contemplating marriage at the age of 26 with less than 3 years' service, and I had no idea what the reaction would be. Anyway, there was no rule against getting engaged, so we put our engagement in the papers and waited to see what happened. Nothing much did happen officially. There was general surprise, and a small amount of consternation, as no one had ever shown signs of challenging the rule before, so there was no precedent to follow. In the end Butterfields were extremely sensible about it. Nothing at all was said by the top brass, and the fact that I was now engaged to be married was simply ignored. The purpose of the rule was to make it easy to post young men from one place to another without having to provide for their wives and children. Those who dutifully obeyed the rule were rewarded, in due course, with extra pay by way of a marriage allowance, plus accommodation and travel for dependants. If I chose to take on a wife at a time when I was supposed to be single, that was up to me, and in the eyes of the firm Deirdre did not exist. So, regarding me as an unencumbered single man, soon after we became engaged they posted me to Japan.

This was a blow, but it was perfectly fair, and there was nothing to be done about it. We had a few weeks' notice and then off I went to Japan to become, they told me, Osaka Shipping Manager, while Deirdre stayed in Hong Kong as a vital cog in the machinery of the so-called War Office. We had no clear plan, except that I would probably serve out the rest of my three-year contract and then we would go home and get married. As it turned out, we hit on a better idea.

Before I left, my fellow jockeys gave Deirdre and me a banquet, organised by Alex Lam – he who called me the last of the amateur jockeys. I wrote from Japan to thank him, and did not expect an answer, but answer he did, and his letter has survived:

"Hong Kong; 25th April 1956
Dear Enfield,
Thank you for writing me your letter of 10th April.
I shall not fail to inform our Novie friends of your gratitude for the simple lunch we gave you before your departure. Hope you have settled down peacefully and comfortably with your new surroundings.

It is indeed a misery to miss you and more so you have been a nice guy to all of us. However, I am sure we shall meet again in one of these days, not far from now. It will be a pleasant things that we can ride together in the early mornings and on those racing days.

As you know, we shall have a meeting with ten races on the 28th. It is hope and always hope that after all we shall be paid with what we have done. May our Novie chaps surprise the old hands!

It will be a great pleasure to hear from you now and then, and meanwhile may I wish you with all my best wishes.
Yours sincerely
Alex Lam."

I was very pleased with this kind letter, and, as he forecast, the time did come when we rode together again in the early mornings and on those racing days.

Chapter 11

Japan

All nations have their quirks and peculiarities, and the Japanese have these in abundance. To me their most remarkable trait is one which I have never seen described elsewhere, and is not altogether easy to put into plain words. In effect, it is that there are things which they understand completely and other things which they do not understand at all. That, you may say, is not uncommon, but the Japanese have an astonishing capacity to move from one to the other – from a state of non-understanding to an absolute mastery of the matter in question. It is almost as if the emperor were, from time to time, to issue a decree that in some area in which his subjects were at present deficient they were, immediately, to become proficient, whereupon they bend their brains to whatever it is and come out on top.

At the time I arrived, they understood ships, which they could build and manage very well, and they understood trains which ran with great efficiency, but they had little idea of roads or cars. The town roads were awful, the potholes enormous, and I had a friend, now deceased, who claimed he was the first man to drive a car from the north to the south of the main island, which he did mostly on a dirt track. The standard Japanese car was the Toyopet, a noisy and supposedly unreliable rattle-trap so despised by the European community that all Europeans had to have cars imported at great cost and subject to a heavy duty, rather than trust themselves to the native product. Then the moment must have come when the emperor ruled, or the Japanese decided, that the time was ripe for them to move from ignorance to expertise, so they started by making good roads in town and fine highways outside, and then they turned their attention to cars. In no time at all they were making better cars than anybody else, and as we know, it was the Japanese who came and rescued the British car industry from extinction.

I had not been there very long when I was given a glimpse of the future by a VIP who arrived on a visit. We were agents for the Blue Funnel Line, of which the parent company was Alfred Holt and Company of Liverpool. Whoever he was, whatever his name, he was in high favour with Alfred Holt and Company, and they said we were to be nice to him, so we were. He revealed the future to us over lunch. His very words were, "Japan is about to become the quality producer of Asia" and he based his prediction on some stuff called grey cloth. I had never heard of grey cloth, but it was evidently the key to everything. He explained that some people grow cotton, some people buy cotton and turn it into grey cloth, and some people buy grey cloth and turn it into finished textiles. If the people who grow cotton decide to stop selling it and to make it into grey cloth for themselves, the former grey-cloth-makers have to go upmarket and switch to making finished textiles. This means the textile makers in turn have to think of something else. The Japanese, he said, having destroyed the British grey cloth industry by making grey cloth more cheaply than it could be done in the UK, had themselves been forced out by the Indians who had started turning their own cotton into grey cloth and making it cheaper still. As a result, the Japanese had moved to making high-quality textiles, but this was just the start, and as time went on they would be forced out of textiles into other areas. Having got the hang of making high quality textiles, they would, in the course of time realise that they needed to learn to make other things of a superior nature, and would in due course become, as he said, the quality producers of Asia.

This may not seem very remarkable now, and at the time it did not strike us as more than an interesting speculation, but how right he was. At the time Japan was still thought of as being a producer of cheap and shoddy goods, and we had no inkling that the wretched Toyopet would become the world beating Toyota, or that the Nikkon camera would come from nowhere to challenge the German Leica. I was told to write to Alfred Holt and Company to report on the visit of their VIP, and perhaps somewhere in their archives is an illuminating forecast of things to come as a result of the Japanese doing their trick of mastering subjects which they had not previously understood, and being better at them than anybody else. I hope, indeed, that Alfred Holt and Company laid down the keels of extra ships to cope with the coming boom, on the strength of my report.

All of which is to jump ahead from what I found when I first arrived. The two largest ports in the south of the island of Honshu are Kobe and Osaka. I was to work in Osaka, but live in Kobe, because that was where all the Europeans lived, so I had to commute to my office daily by train.

I have said that they understood trains in Japan, and there was nothing wrong with the Japanese trains, but there were far too many Japanese people wanting to use them. At least there were too many who wanted to shuttle between Kobe and Osaka every day. Each train arrived exactly on time. There were marks on the platform to show where the carriage doors would be, and every train stopped with the doors exactly opposite the marks. We commuters did not straggle along the platform as if we were in England, but formed up in solid blocks opposite the marks. As the doors opened we surged forward and fought for seats, tooth and nail. When the carriage was full beyond what could reasonably be called capacity, with some people on the platform still shoving and wriggling in the hope of getting in, the doors would slam shut trapping a few arms and legs in the process. There were guards on the platform whose duty was to push as hard as they could at the back of the scrum, and then to wrench down and shove in any limbs that got stuck in the doors.

It was rare for me to get a seat. I do not think I was sufficiently ruthless, and lacked the stomach for all-out combat, so I usually had to stand, hanging onto an overhead strap. I believe that in the Land of the Rising Sun the people have since changed their eating habits and have grown taller in later generations, but at five foot eight inches I was taller than the average Japanese of those days. This meant that I stood with the top of a Japanese head, always thickly smeared with Brylcreem, at about the level of my nose. It seemed that most of my fellow travellers had breakfasted on a root called daikon, a sort of Oriental garlic, so the sensation for me was exactly that of a sardine packed in Brylcreem flavoured with garlic, and it lasted for half an hour. I made this journey, there and back, six days a week. Still, the human spirit is equipped to deal with adversity. In some surprising bookshop with a small selection of English books I found a World's Classics copy of the Canterbury Tales. Clutching a strap in one hand, and holding Chaucer above the level of the Brylcreemed heads, I read all of these admirable poems during the 15 months that I was making the journey.

As we poured into Kobe station in the morning there were always hordes of little Japanese children being moved from one place to another, rather like sheep being herded from one grazing ground to the next. They all wore navy blue sailor suits, and you could tell the boys from the girls because the boys wore shorts and the girls skirts, but otherwise to our eyes they were all the same. We wondered whether this mass movement of tiny, seemingly identical creatures was managed without loss or whether, as one of us put it, they allowed a small percentage for wastage.

When I got to the office I sat at my desk surrounded by Japanese. Upstairs there were four other Swire people doing different things, but downstairs I was the only foreigner, this being the term the locals used to describe us Europeans. To my right was the big, imposing Tada san who was called, I think, Office Manager. I was nominally, and Tada san actually, in charge of everything that went on. To my left was Sally san, who took dictation on such occasions as I needed to write a letter. Scattered about there were perhaps a dozen or sixteen clerks called This san or That san, some young, some elderly, some male, some female. They dealt with paperwork, or they accepted bookings by telephone, or else they visited the merchants of Osaka to canvass for cargos for our ships. The results of these visits they reported to Tada san, who consolidated it all into a statement of the space to be reserved for us on ships loading in Kobe or Osaka and this, with Sally san's help, I passed on to Hong Kong by telegram, neither adding a jot nor subtracting a tittle from the figures put before me.

The Japanese, being at the fine textile stage of their development, were major importers of Australian wool. When it was a matter of exporting goods from Japan, it was the exporters who decided which ships to use, but when it came to importing wool from Australia, the importers made the decision. Accordingly we had a man called Morioka san who went about among the wool importers trying to persuade them to choose our ships rather than those of our competitors. Morioka san's conversation was of Tops, of Nolls and of Greasy Wool, these being, I gathered, technical terms of the wool trade. From time to time he presented me with statements of the quantities of these mysterious substances which we expected to obtain for our ships loading in Australia, and these I passed on by telegram to Sydney, again contributing nothing of my own to the process. I seemed to be no more than a cypher, but this did not matter as the ships came from Australia and left from Japan always tolerably well loaded and sometimes absolutely full, so I found myself in charge of a successful undertaking while contributing almost nothing to success itself.

As well as signing a great many bills of lading, as in Hong Kong, I had also to add my signature to a regular flow of cargo claim forms. Cargoes in those days did not travel in big containers, but generally came alongside in small boats called lighters, to be lifted up by cranes and stowed in the holds under the eye of a ship's officer. From time to time something got dropped or wetted or otherwise damaged, and this was a risk against which shippers always insured. To claim on any insurance policy they needed my signature on a piece of paper, which I think was a statement to the effect that the damage was due to an unfortunate accident and nobody's fault whatever.

I grasped the principle, and there was nothing difficult about signing, so I signed away freely except for one occasion when I must have thought it strange that all these accidents kept happening without anyone being to blame. Thinking that perhaps occasionally somebody might have blundered, I looked into the circumstances of one particular claim, concluded that it was the shipper's own silly fault, and withheld my signature. This provoked an agonised letter from Showa Unyu Kaisha Ltd which is one of the few memorabilia that have survived from those times. It read as follows:

"It is dare day, not right right your claim to us that we must have responsibility, on the contrary, we have a confidence that we had completed our operation wit the procdent handling not to arise any damage, as a result this dameges was occurred in the corse heavy logs, It is a Act of God, so generally in Osaka port these damages does not hold responsibility for the cost of repairing the damege and if other matter must be hold responsibility of corse, any way."

I was so delighted with this letter that I signed their claim form immediately. Also I realised that the only thing I could possibly achieve by behaving in this way was to antagonise some of our customers, so after that I signed whatever was put before me without making any further difficulties.

So much for my office. I was living in a little wooden house in a suburb of Kobe, with a sweet elderly cook called Oba san, a pretty maid called Kazuko san and a pregnant Akita dog called Maia san. An Akita, for those who have not met the breed, is something like a smaller blond Alsatian or German Shepherd. The establishment properly belonged to someone else who was on leave at the time, and all I had to do was move in as a temporary tenant. It was extremely luxurious. Oba san was an excellent cook and a good source of entertainment. On the day when she bought some live crabs in the fish market and they escaped in the train on the way back she laughed so much she could hardly get the story out. Kazuko san was very decorative, kept the house spotless, did my washing and waited at table. Maia san's contribution was, in due time, to produce a litter of pedigree Akita puppies, which were very sweet and about which I had to do nothing as Oba san and Kazuko san looked after them. I have never lived in such style, before or since. It was, of course, rather expensive as I had to pay Oba san and Kazuko san their wages, which they received with much bowing once a month, and I had to meet the cost of escaping crabs and any other food or drink, but the costs of the house were covered by my employers.

Before long, Deirdre arrived. She had come to the end of her tour with the so-called War Office, and they owed her three months leave. We planned that she should spend this in Japan, but it wasn't very satisfactory. First of all, there was a difficulty as to where she should stay. Nowadays of course she would have lived with me, but in those days young ladies did not cohabit with their fiancés so I found her a room in a house fairly near mine. It was not a good room, being hot and uncomfortable and vaguely frightening, so she got a better one by going to the nearest Catholic priest and ordering him to solve the problem. He was, as I recall, a Dutchman, and was at first inclined to think that re-housing Deirdre was not part of his duties, but she had leverage. By this I mean that she threatened to move in with me if he didn't get on with it, so he found her a much better room in the house of one of his converts, in order to save her from the deadly sin of fornication.

Even so, it wasn't much fun for her, hanging about by herself while I was off signing bills of lading and cargo claim forms, so our next thought was that perhaps she could get a job and we could afford to get married. She did get a job, but it was a nasty job in a stuffy office with some unpleasant Americans and a unisex lavatory, so she gave it up. Then we arrived at the simple and obvious solution, that we should get married but behave as people behave in England. I should go to work and Deirdre should cook and look after the house. Everyone else employed at least a cook-amah and if not a cook and an amah. Those who had children had an amah to look after them, and the children learnt Japanese by osmosis from their amahs and used to discuss things between themselves in that language when they wanted to keep their parents in the dark. We would manage without an amah, but I hasten to say that this did not mean that we had to get rid of the wonderful Oba san and the pretty Kazuko san. We stayed on with them in the little wooden house until its rightful tenant came back from leave, and then we moved to a vacant flat in Kobe where we could suit ourselves as to how we lived.

So we got married, twice, each time to each other, and each time on the same day. As Deirdre is a Catholic she needed to be married in a Catholic church, but in a pagan country such as Japan a church wedding has no force in law, so we had to have a preliminary marriage conducted by the British Consul. Getting married was a new experience for us, and marrying people was a new experience for him. Thinking to give the ceremony a bit of colour he got a Union Flag and draped it over his office desk, which made it look exactly like the coffin of someone about to be buried at sea. Then, having become man and wife in a ceremony conducted over a coffin, we separated to meet again later at the Catholic church to be married once more by an extremely nice French missionary. Somebody took a cine film which shows Tada san in a smart suit and Mrs Tada in a beautiful kimono, and the irrepressible Oba san doubled up with laughter as we were pelted with rice on leaving the church.

After the ceremony we said to the priest "We hope you can come to the reception."

"Alas, no," he said, in his French way. "I cannot. I am busy. *Perhaps next time?*"

I am happy to say there has not been a next time and we are still man and wife after fifty eight years.

Everybody was wonderfully kind. My boss and his wife gave us the reception at their house, attended by twenty people. Deirdre had a very pretty bridesmaid in the tiny daughter of a colleague. By some miracle Oswald Cheung turned up on holiday from Hong Kong and was co-opted as best man.

We had lots of telegrams from family and friends, and my fellow jockey T L Wong, who had persuaded me to buy some life insurance, wrote as follows:

AMERICAN INTERNATIONAL ASSURANCE CO., LTD.
(INCORPORATED UNDER THE COMPANIES ORDINANCES OF HONGKONG)

AMERICAN INTERNATIONAL BUILD:
12-14 QUEEN'S ROAD, CENTRAL
HONG KONG

Butterfield & Swire, 23rd Aug, 1956.
Osaka, Japan. (Branch)

Dear Mr. E.R.Enfield
Let me tender my hearty congratulations, and with you every blessing wedded life. My and my friend's name were jointed the groop of gifts of a big medal of silver, which was send you by many friends of Hongkong Jokey Club. May I inform you that your inc premium of qaurterly figue US$46.40 _ HK$278.50 Please send to our company before end of Aug.

Sincerely Yours
T. L. Wong

That evening we flew to Tokyo and were whisked in the head man's car up to the area of Lake Hakone for a short honeymoon.

We stayed at two hotels and we went back on a visit forty seven years later, so my recollection has been refreshed. The Fujiya is a spa hotel which was originally built of wood, was extended in wood, and of wood it remains. From the cedar-panelled reception area you go down panelled corridors to your room, passing pictures of distinguished people who have been there before, such as Pandit Nehru and Crown Prince Gustavus Adolphus of Sweden. On our return trip they showed us the page in the register where, on August 16th 1956 I had signed us in as Mr and Mrs Enfield for the first time in our lives. The fifth entry after ours was Carlo Ponti, husband of Sophia Loren, so you can see it was a pretty superior place. I remember waking up on honeymoon to the sound of running water, and you still do. It comes from the Japanese garden where streams cascade from rocks into pools full of huge contented-looking goldfish. Inside all the hot water, including that in your bathroom, has bubbled up hot out of the ground.

The other hotel, the Hakone, has been pulled down and rebuilt since our honeymoon. As a newlywed, I thought it part of my morning duty to leap out of bed and draw back the curtains so that my wife could enjoy the view of Lake Hakone without getting up. On our second visit I found a button marked "drapes" so I pushed it to see what happened and the curtains miraculously parted to reveal the snow-covered peak of Fuji san, the great mountain, glistening beyond the lake. I may say that the Japanese are now absolutely at the cutting edge of bedroom technology – we had to send for Room Service to explain the mysteries of the bathwater, and the loo had a heated seat plus a control panel beside it with ten buttons. I did not dare to push any of them for fear of what it might do.

I cannot say that Japan in 1956 was an ideal place to start married life, particularly for Deirdre, as she was left alone for much of the time. This was either because I was at the office by day or because I was suffering the miseries of Japanese entertainment by night. The latter needs some explanation.

Japan was a strictly masculine society. If a married couple were out together the man would walk in front and the woman trot along behind. I remember seeing Tada san take off his jacket on a hot day and hand it to his wife who obediently accepted it and walked in his wake with his coat over her arm. This being the general attitude, men were often asked out and wives never. All such invitations were a matter of corporate hospitality. We never made any Japanese friends or set foot in a private Japanese house, but the stevedores who loaded our ships were painfully hospitable and kept inviting the Butterfield men to parties. As well as being very hospitable our hosts were also, in my view, extremely boring.

This was an unfortunate combination, as to be boring but inhospitable is perfectly blameless, and to be hospitable and amusing is definitely good, but to be boring and hospitable at the same time is a tiresome combination. I may be doing them an injustice. I spoke no Japanese, and so I am in no position to complain that their English was elementary. Possibly in their own language their conversation sparkled, but in English it was at best juvenile, and to keep the conversation going through a long evening was a desperate business.

You are to picture Deirdre alone at night while I was out with some other Butterfields men and a bunch of Japanese at a geisha party. You may think it reasonable that Deirdre might worry as to what I was getting up to, but there was nothing for her to worry about unless she could conjure up some sympathy for the fact that I was bored stiff.

To those who know nothing about it, a geisha party may suggest a wild night in a brothel, but it is not like that at all. The Japanese are very keen on baths, and if the party took place somewhere there was a bath, you started with a bath and spent the rest of the occasion wearing a cotton Japanese dressing gown called a yukata. If there was no bath you sat it out in your office suit on the floor, as the Japanese do not believe in furniture in general, or chairs in particular. In an otherwise empty room the only concession to the idea of furniture is a low table, and you sit round that, drinking sake out of tiny cups. Sake, which is generally described as a rice wine, is pleasant enough when they warm it up, and is served out of tiny cups which are constantly filled by twittering giggling geisha girls. The girls kneel beside you, and the cups are tiny because Japanese men like to be waited on by kneeling girls, and if the cups were bigger they would not have to be filled so often, so the men would not be waited on so much, which would not be such fun.

Also, you get a meal. In those days the Japanese had a way of producing superb ingredients and using them to create disgusting meals. Geisha parties always included a dish called sukiyaki. My memory may not be entirely reliable, but if I were asked for a recipe for sukiyaki I would say, take a selection of root vegetables and some strips of fatty beef, parboil the whole in front of the guests and serve with a raw egg. If you can imagine yourself choking down strings of parboiled beef fat which you have managed to pick up with wooden chopsticks, you will have an idea of one aspect of a geisha party. The food is somehow made worse by the obvious thought that if only they had trimmed the fat off the beef and grilled it, fried the eggs and cooked the vegetables properly, it would all have been delicious.

After the eating, the girls, who are dressed in very pretty kimonos but are not usually very pretty themselves, put on an entertainment. One or more of them plays a sort of banjo called a samisen and the others dance about and sing. I, of course, never had any idea of what they were singing about, and the dancing is nothing special, but they were doing their best to please so we all did our best to seem pleased, and applauded heartily. Then there are party games, a sort of pale imitation of a mess night in the army, only in this case they involve elementary charades or little playlets, sometimes of a rather coarse nature, which is the nearest thing there is to any kind of impropriety in the whole occasion. After the games you are allowed, mercifully, to go home.

I must not give the impression that the only terrible entertainment was that inflicted by the Japanese. Butterfields themselves had a way of putting on terrible parties on board their ships. The fare was beer and sandwiches, or the equivalent, and the guests were either Japanese or Indian merchants, there being a great many of the latter. I noticed in my time in the East that Indians are astonishing linguists. Everywhere I went there were Indian merchants carrying on their business in the language of the country – in Cantonese in Hong Kong, in Japanese in Japan and in Thai in Thailand. They all spoke English as well, which on these shipboard social occasions helped in making conversation through a long evening with people whom one hardly knew. I suppose they must have enjoyed themselves as they kept accepting our invitations, but as it was common practice among all the shipping companies to entertain in this way, they sometimes got confused as to which one was the host on any particular occasion. I remember a bearded Sikh demanding silence and starting off, "We wish to thank Messrs Dodwells ...." only to be shouted down with a chorus of, "Not Dodwells, you fool – Butterfields!"

Business entertaining apart, the low point in the Kobe social calendar was Burns Night. Charles Lamb had the temerity to say, "I have been trying all my life to like Scotchmen, and am obliged to desist from the experiment in despair." You cannot get away with things like that nowadays, but perhaps I can go so far as to say that Burns Night brings out the worst in expatriate Scots, of whom there were a good many in Kobe.

It is quite a bogus occasion. I am not a great admirer of Burns the poet – some are, some aren't, – but I suspect that few Scots have read much of his work and that many have not read him at all. Nonetheless they profess to admire him very much, and on Burns Night they go in for an orgy in his honour. If they possibly can, they dress up in kilts. Men who would never wear such a garment in the normal course of things, wear one on Burns Night. There are those who have never owned a kilt, and have come to Japan without a kilt, and when Burns Night looms they send home for kilts to be flown out, and are on tenterhooks until they arrive. There is a small shamefaced minority who come in dinner jackets, but kilts are the thing.

Then they make dirty jokes. Although they know little about Burns they think he was a lecherous fellow, so there is a fund of grubby jokes about Robbie Burns which they fire off on Burns night. They drink too much whisky and they eat haggis. In Kobe the haggis was brought in with much pomp, preceded by a man holding two crossed whisky bottles above his head, and loudly cheered by the kilted throng. They only eat a little haggis though, as it is such a disgusting dish, and it is distributed in minute portions, to be choked down as quickly as possible and flushed away with whisky. They manage to carry on like this till late into the night. Now Deirdre and I, of course, had not the least objection to Scotsmen going in for Burns Nights. They could have had a Burns Night twice a week for all we cared if only they had not insisted on inviting us. But they did, and such were the social pressures that we lacked the courage to refuse, so we suffered such occasions not once but twice.

But life was by no means without its pleasures. For one thing, we had a superb Christmas. According to the accepted theory Christmas is a family affair, but we were separated from our families by thousands and thousands of miles. Nobody invited us to join their private family gatherings, so there was no one but us. We came down in the morning to find Oba san and Kazuko san beautifully dressed in their best kimonos, with Maia san and all the puppies wearing pink ribbons round their necks – an effect with which Oba san was enormously pleased. She cooked us a proper Christmas dinner, and before that we went for a walk. I am slightly ashamed at saying it, but Deirdre and I agree that of all the Christmases of our married life, that one in Japan with neither children nor parents nor other relations, but with Oba san and Kazuko san to look after us, with a peaceful walk on a cold clear day, was quite the best of our lives.

There was a station nearby where you could catch a stopping train towards Osaka, and there were a great many places along the way where you could get off and almost at once find yourself out among paddy fields and farms and hills and woods and rivers. As walking country, Japan of those days was the best I have ever come across. It was exceedingly beautiful, definitely Oriental, in a willow-pattern sort of way, well provided with tracks and paths, and we more or less had it to ourselves. We might meet an occasional farmer, and once we came upon a man who grew flowers and sent us home with a big bunch of chrysanthemums: "My presento you," he said with a huge grin. Such people you might encounter, but we never, ever, came across any other walkers. I have said that there was a sharp distinction between the things the Japanese understood and the things they did not. They had grasped the idea of beauty spots, to which they flocked in their hundreds and left the ground covered in bento boxes, little wooden boxes in which they brought picnics of cold rice and raw fish. Walking, on the other hand, was a notion that was entirely foreign to them, so they never went in for it. I suspect that that has now changed. When we went back we saw shops something like those you find in the English Lake District, where you can kit yourself up with boots and knapsacks, and probably breeches and alpenstocks, and set about walking in a serious manner. Furthermore, to our great regret we found that the little rural stops along the railway have been swamped with building, and our efforts at finding the places where we used to walk ended in failure.

When the proper tenant of the little wooden house came back from leave, we moved into a cosy modern flat in Kobe. Deirdre learnt to cook, which she hadn't done before, and to shop in Japanese, and to answer the telephone by repeating the number in Japanese, "haji rokku nanna ichi" or something like that. The bachelor upstairs had a pretty amah called Michiko san, with whom Deirdre got on extremely well. Michiko san kindly took on full responsibility for stoking the hot water boiler which supplied both flats, and employed her feminine charms to get the man who brought the groceries to chop up the kindling wood. There was a little garden in which we entertained friends to a version of clock golf which had something of the character of snooker, because, in order to make the most of the confined space, you had to canon the balls off the garden wall. The laundryman made us a present of a mongrel puppy which he found wandering in the street and delivered to us on a piece of string. Someone else gave us a kitten, and the puppy and the kitten played together interminably.

As well as jogging along like this, we did the proper tourist things. We watched girls diving for oysters at a pearl fishery and we saw men fishing with cormorants on strings and tight collars round their throats. We went to beauty spots and admired the temples and the cherry blossom, and tried to disregard the bento boxes. We went once to the Kabuki Theatre where the costumes were magnificent and one scene as gloriously memorable as anything I have seen in a theatre anywhere. The hero was stalking along at night, lighting his way with a lantern, while eight evil-looking assassins lurked beside the path. They leapt out at him; he threw down the lantern and plunged the theatre in darkness; there was a great clashing of swords; he relit his lantern; all the assassins were dead and he stalked off to huge cheers.

*

One of our simple pleasures was to wander round the great Dai Maru department store. This was built on several floors and you went from one to the next by escalator. At either end of each escalator was a pair of girls in beautiful kimonos, and as you stepped on at the bottom the first pair of girls bowed and said, "Arrigato gozai masu" which means "Thank you very much!" When you reached the top, the second pair of girls bowed and they too said, "Arrigato gozai masu." So, having been thanked for having been so kind as to get on the escalator at the bottom, you were thanked again for taking the trouble to get off at the top. When we went on our return visit we hurried round to the Dai Maru to ride on the escalators, but found, to our great disappointment, that the Arrigato girls had been abolished. Not that it was much of a job for a girl, but it was a colourful example of the exquisite politeness of which the Japanese nation is capable.

Towards the end of my three-year tour John Swire and Sons sprang an agreeable surprise. They had revised their rules, they said, and concluded that they were lagging behind the times. Perhaps it was rather hard to make their young men wait for seven years before they could marry, so they had decided to make it three. As I had jumped the gun, from three years to the day when I stepped on an aeroplane at Heathrow bound for Hong Kong, I would become a fully respectable married man with a recognised wife and a handsome addition to my salary. All they asked in return was that we should not go on leave at once, but go to Hong Kong where I would spend a few months helping to shuffle the ships of the Butterfield fleet around the South China Sea and the South Pacific. We were quite pleased at this idea, so we readily agreed. I was to fill in for someone on leave and he, being a friend, most kindly lent us his car while he was away. I got out my jodhpurs, unpacked my boots and silk breeches, applied for a rider's badge and re-appeared at the Jockey Club. My return there was noticed by the Chinese racing paper in the following paragraph, as translated for me by Tsoi Ning:

Extract of "Fat Choy Pony News"
Enfield is working for B. & S. and lived in the firm's Mess in the Peak. Years ago, he usually took a bicycle down to the valley for the morning gallops. Last year he was posted to a B. & S. branch office in Japan, where he married Miss Jenkins. They both enjoy a happy married life, and live harmoniously like fish in the water! He is now back in the B. & S. Hong Kong Office. Therefore he can make his appearance in the Racing Course again. He is now a married man. He also has a car to go around places.

After four months in Hong Kong we went on home leave and then to Bangkok.

Chapter 12

Almost a Diplomatic Incident

The Bangkok office of Cathay Pacific Airways consisted, firstly, of three Thai girls who sat at the counter and sold tickets. (I call them Thai, though in those days they were more often called Siamese.) One of them was exceptionally efficient and the other two were bright enough. Then there was a Siamese office manager who, I later discovered, was given to stealing the cash. Also there was a Chinese sales manager whose job was to drum up business in the large Chinese community of Bangkok. He had a business card with Chinese writing on one side, and on the other the words "Kingsweet Y.T. Chen."

"Why Kingsweet?" I asked.

"It is my foreign name," he said, making it plain that this, to him, was a complete explanation. However, nobody ever called him Kingsweet and to most people he was known as Y.T. and Mr Chen to the girls. Y.T. had an assistant called Lena Wong, and there was an office boy, and then there was a secretary, Miss Thavee, who was a sort of a princess. This did not mean quite all that it sounds, partly because the king used to have a great many wives, and partly because the Thais kept their titles going to the third generation. Miss Thavee's title was Mom Rajawongse, which meant that she was the great granddaughter of a king. I noticed that Thai visitors to the office treated her with great respect, putting their hands together and bowing very politely and it was explained to me that she was descended from one of the king's more important wives, which was reflected in her status in society. She was neither plain nor beautiful, but extremely nice, and a bit older than me, say 32 to my 28. My predecessor called her Tweetie, which did not suit her at all, as she was tall and shy, but I fell into the habit of calling her Tweetie myself before I realised that Kuhn Thavee would probably have been better. She was Kuhn Thavee to the rest of the staff, but she did not seem to mind being Tweetie to me.

At that time the Swire Group owned the whole of Cathay Pacific Airways. Deirdre and I went on leave, expecting to go back to Hong Kong, but a letter came from John Swire & Sons saying, in effect, this: "There has been a change of plan. You are to go to Bangkok to take over the Cathay Pacific office. Come to Hong Kong for a two week crash course on how to run an airline, and then go and do it."

So we went to Hong Kong and they taught me two things. The first is that the air is not free, or at least it was not then, though things may have changed a bit. The sea is free, by which I mean that a Norwegian ship can dock in Liverpool and load a cargo for Buenos Aires without asking permission of anyone. The air, they said, is different. Air traffic is a matter of bilateral agreements between governments by which it might be agreed, for example, that both British Airways and Air France may carry passengers and cargo between Paris and London. Everything, they said, is governed by these bilaterals.

The other thing they said was that they had bought a new aeroplane. Cathay Pacific in those days was not the enormous enterprise that it is today, but was more like an airborne local bus service. They had owned, up to that point, three aeroplanes in all, a DC3, a DC4 and a DC6. I forget what the DC3 did, but the bulk of the business consisted in flights between Hong Kong, Bangkok and Singapore with the DC4 and the DC6. Adding an extra aeroplane, in this case a DC6B, meant a great increase in the number of flights and a complete revision of the previous schedules.

About this, they said, I was not to worry. Everything had been arranged. All the new schedules had been published and all I had to do was go to Bangkok and let it happen. So I went to Bangkok and very shortly got involved in what was very nearly a diplomatic incident.

I took over from a man I did not care for. He was a strange fellow, sometimes speaking with a false American accent as if he had a small part in a play by Tennessee Williams, and sometimes wearing a monocle and talking like Noel Coward. I do not know what he was interested in, but I don't think it was Cathay Pacific. He had the reputation among the other airline managers of never buying a round of drinks, and I was glad when he went away.

So there we were, this little group of people, with no one to bother us or to help us. No one else in Bangkok was employed by John Swire &

Sons, and I was the only European, with my boss in Hong Kong. I was still at the stage of finding my way about and working out how I could be most useful in what I was supposed to do, when, one day, Miss Thavee came into my office and handed me a letter.

It was from Air Marshall Chalerm of the Royal Thai Air Force. I do not remember the exact words but it was brief and to the point, and the message was this: *"I, Air Marshall Chalerm, have considered the proposal of you, Cathay Pacific Airways, to operate additional flights in and out of Bangkok and I do not agree."*

That was awkward. All the new schedules had been sent to travel agents and other airlines, we were busily accepting bookings and so were the people in Hong Kong and Singapore. The shiny new DC6B was due to make its first landing at Bangkok airport in just over two weeks' time, but civil aviation in Thailand was in the hands of the Royal Thai Air Force, and if Air Marshall Chalerm said he wasn't having it, then it was off.

We used to communicate with Hong Kong by teleprinter, so Miss Thavee teleprinted off a copy of the Air Marshall's letter and back, with all possible speed, came the answer: "Go at once to the embassy, look up the bilateral, and get them to tell the Thai government they cannot do this."

I got into my car, drove to the embassy, parked in the road outside, and at the gate came up against a Royal Marine guard. I explained to him as best I could that I needed the help of the embassy because the Thai government would not let us, Cathay Pacific, land our aeroplanes in Bangkok as often as we wanted. The Royal Marine, having digested this, decided that it was a matter for the most junior official of all, known as the Third Secretary, and escorted me to the Third Secretary's office and ushered me in.

As soon as I set eyes on him I said, "Oh hello, I recognise you. You were at Oxford. You read classics. We went to the same lectures."

"I know your face," he replied "nice to see you. What are you doing in Bangkok? This is rather a strange place to meet!"

"Yes indeed," said I, "and since you ask, I am here with Cathay Pacific."

"Well, well," said the Third Secretary, or words to that effect, and so we spent some time reminiscing on the old days and getting up-to-date on the present days as if we were bosom friends, although we had never spoken before that moment.

Eventually we got down to business and I explained for the second time that day that I had this problem with aeroplanes which were in danger of landing without any landing rights.

"I see," said the Third Secretary. "I will go to the library and get the bilateral, and we will have a look at it." Off he went, and back he came in a matter of minutes with the bilateral in his hand.

It proved to be a magnificent document. To all appearances it had been drawn up personally by the sovereigns of the two nations concerned. It set out in dignified terms the details of the agreement reached between Her Royal Britannic Majesty and His Royal Thai Majesty almost as if Queen Elizabeth II and King Bhumibol Adulyadej had hammered it out between them in the library at Balmoral.

There was an English and a Thai version, and while the Third Secretary did not venture to interpret the Thai, when we got down to the English we could see a difficulty. I am not certain, but I think the key word was "consult." The bilateral gave both Cathay Pacific and Thai Airways a general right to fly between Hong Kong and Bangkok, but if at any time either party wished to increase the number of flights above the level then current, such party was to consult the other party beforehand. I could see that the Cathay Pacific line would be, "You have a right to be consulted, but you do not have a right of veto" while the Thai line would be, "It does not mean that you must consult us but can take no notice of what we say." As the airport at which Cathay Pacific wished to land belonged to His Royal Thai Majesty it seemed to me that they had the stronger hand.

"I think," said the Third Secretary after careful consideration, "that this is one for the Air Attaché."

He led me down the corridor and introduced me to the Air Attaché in the form of an out-of-uniform Squadron Leader. For the third time that day I explained my difficulty and then the Third Secretary joined in with an exposition of the contents of the bilateral.

"I see," said the Air Attaché. He thought for a moment, and then he said, "I will go and see Chalerm."

He thought for a moment more, and then added, "I think I will go in uniform." Then he gave it a little more thought and said, "I think I will wear my sword."

"Oh, that is excellent," I said. "Thank you so much," and went away full of confidence. I had this picture in my mind of the Air Attaché pacing through the corridors of the Thai Air Ministry in the full panoply of the RAF dress uniform, with his sword clanking at his side. Obviously this was the way to get things done in Bangkok diplomatic circles, and the problem was as good as solved.

Two or three days went by without any message from the embassy, so I rang the Air Attaché.

"Did you manage to see the Air Marshall?" I asked.

"Oh yes," he said.

"How did you get on?"

"They don't agree," he said.

He spoke as if that was that. He had done his stuff, been to see the Air Marshall, and had now moved on to other, possibly weightier matters. I thanked him and rang off. In the interval I had been through the files and thought I might have got to the root of the difficulty. As far as I could see, my predecessor, he of the monocle and the funny voice, had not done anything at all by way of consultation. He had fired off a general letter to all the travel agents and airlines in Bangkok giving details of all the extra flights and revised schedules that we intended to operate, and at the foot of this letter were the words *copy to Civil Aviation personnel*. That was all and there was no covering letter or anything else by way of prior notice on the file.

This struck me as a pretty casual way of carrying on, and if the Thai authorities had taken offence, then they could not really be blamed. Perhaps, I thought, if I go and grovel a bit, the damage can be undone. Accordingly I asked Miss Thavee if she could make an appointment for me to see Air Marshall Chalerm myself.

Of course so great a man was not going to grant me an immediate audience, but he agreed to see me in three days' time, at two o'clock in the afternoon. On that day I presented myself at the Royal Thai Air Ministry at five to two and was shown to a seat in a corridor. There I was kept waiting for half an hour, as is to be expected when a superior person such as an Air Marshall is about to grant an audience to a supplicant such as me. Finally the door of his office was opened and I was shown in.

The Air Marshall's office, as I remember it, was extremely long, the far end being a good many yards from the entrance. Right at the end was a very big desk, and behind the desk, facing the door, was a very large man in a blue uniform, wearing very large horn-rimmed glasses which made him look like an enormous frog. I crossed the intervening yards of office space, and when I arrived at the desk I said, "Good afternoon, Air Marshall."

He gave no reply, nor did he indicate by the least twitch of an eyelid that this remark had registered with him.

There was a chair by his desk, and he did not indicate that I should sit on it, but I sat on it anyway. Then I said, "I am very grateful to you for seeing me, Air Marshall." To this he said nothing, but stared at me impassively from behind the enormous glasses. There being nothing else for it, I plunged into my prepared speech which went something like this:

"I very much regret, Air Marshall, that this difficulty has arisen in connection with our proposed new schedules. I have been most carefully through the files, and I was distressed to see that the procedures for consultation laid down in the bilateral seem not to have been followed correctly. I can only say that no discourtesy was intended and I would like to promise you that this is so. It was, I can assure you, simply an oversight. Nevertheless, I do, on behalf of my company, most sincerely apologise."

I paused at this point, hoping that he might like to join in, but he didn't. Instead he continued to gaze at me in silence, and it felt as if the frog's tongue might lick out and eat me at any moment. I struggled gamely on.

"You did not specify any particular points in your letter which you felt needed clarification, but if there are any such matters, then of course my company ...." And so on and on until I ran out breath, or argument, or just got desperate, but anyway I stopped.

The Air Marshall said nothing and I could think of nothing more to say, so we sat in silence for a long 15 seconds. Then for the first and only time the great man spoke. "We do not agree," he said.

I went back and reported failure to Hong Kong. We were now almost within a week of the start of the new schedules, and while it would be wrong to say there was a bit of a panic in head office, this was only wrong because my boss, whose name was Duncan Bluck never, in any circumstances, panicked. All the same, he did show signs of anxiety in the form of a teleprinter message next day saying, "I am coming down. Book me a hotel and an appointment with the ambassador."

I was about to open negotiations with the Third Secretary, when the door of my office opened. In came Miss Thavee. Clearly she was bearing news of some importance.

"I have had a call from the Air Ministry" she said.

"Now what?" I asked.

"They say they agree."

I looked at her in astonishment. "Tweetie, are you quite sure?"

"Yes" she said. "They are sending a letter."

I have said that Miss Thavee was a shy person, and it seemed to me that she was looking extremely embarrassed. "Tweetie" I said "what did you do?"

At this she looked even more embarrassed. "Oh," she confessed hesitantly, "I rang them up. I said that you had only just got here, and that none of this was your fault. And that you were only a young man. And that they were making it very difficult for you. And couldn't they just agree?" To which the answer, I gathered, was, "Oh well, as it's you, all right."

I could see that Tweetie was extremely worried that I might say that it was no part of her duties to meddle in matters of this sort, but I said no such thing. I congratulated her warmly and thanked her heartily. Apart from relief at being off the hook I was fascinated at the way things seemed to be done in Bangkok. Evidently if you happen to be the great granddaughter of one of the king's more important wives, you could pull rank on an Air Marshall and succeed where the British Embassy failed. Or else perhaps Air Marshall Chalerm was her cousin - I never enquired, not wishing to embarrass her further.

Anyway, sure enough, within hours a motorcyclist arrived from the ministry with a letter saying, in effect, that the Air Marshall had further considered our proposal and raised no objection. We teleprinted this to

Duncan Bluck in Hong Kong. Duncan was the most efficient man I ever worked with, economical both of his time and his words, so back came the laconic message "Well done!" I then enjoyed dictating to Tweetie a letter saying that it was kind of him to congratulate me but that actually we were only rescued from the scrape into which we had got by means of a judicious phone call made by Miss Thavee to her contact in the Air Ministry.

Before we left Bangkok 14 months later, Cathay Pacific once again bought one more aeroplane and again proposed to increase the number of flights in and out of Bangkok. Looking back, I am surprised that no one in head office sent me down a carefully drafted letter to be sent to the Air Ministry, but they didn't. They didn't even remind me to write such a letter myself, they just left it to me. Perhaps part of the enormous success of the Swire organisation may be that, having once given you a job, they leave you to get on with it.

Anyway, I could see that I had to walk a fine line in order to leave the way open for discussion without seeming to seek permission, as I must not appear to acknowledge that permission was something we required. Bearing in mind the magnificent language in which the bilateral was couched, I thought perhaps a flowery turn of phrase might be appropriate, and cast my mind back to the time when I was a National Service officer cadet. In those days, to apply for a weekend's leave you had to write to the adjutant in a prescribed form which started with the words "Sir, I have the honour to submit this my application…" That sounded just about right for an Air Marshall, so as far as I remember my letter went like this:

"To Air Marshall Chalerm
Air Marshall, the Royal Thai Air Force
Sir:
I have the honour to submit herewith the schedules which my company proposes to operate from the 1st August next. Should there be anything herein which you would wish to discuss, I shall, of course, be happy to make myself available, and remain
Sir ... ..."

Remain what? I was so carried away with this sort of lingo that I was tempted to remain his Obedient Humble Servant, but it seemed to be going a bit far, so I think I settled for remaining his truly. Anyway it worked, as we had no difficulty and there was no need for Tweetie to make one of her telephone calls, which was just as well as by that time she had left to get married.

Chapter 13

Bangkok

If you had wanted to draw up a list of things wrong with Bangkok in 1958, as a sort of catalogue of reasons to keep clear of the place, you could have made a formidable case against the so-called Venice of the East. They were all reasons of a physical nature, some of which people warned us about before we got there, while some struck us as soon as we arrived and others we discovered as we went along. As we had wanted to go back to Hong Kong and had no wish to go to Bangkok anyway, we arrived in a pretty discontented frame of mind, but when the time came for us to leave, the photographs taken at the airport all showed Deirdre in sunglasses, which she wore in an effort to hide the fact that she was in tears at the prospect of parting.

Some of the disadvantages have, at a distance, a certain picturesque quality, though not, I think, the climate, especially if you do not like the heat, which Deirdre doesn't. Bangkok is hot at all times, usually 30 degrees or more. Stepping out of an aeroplane at the airport is like stepping into an oven. Stepping into a parked car was like stepping into an over-heated oven, and cars in those days were not air conditioned. Mostly it is hot and dry, but for a short time it is hot and wet. When it was wet the canals, which they called klongs, used to overflow and we found that we had fish flopping about on our lawn, which I suppose you could think was picturesque.

I have to say, though, in defence of this climate, that provided you could shelter from the rain you were not likely to die of exposure, and as rice and bananas grew abundantly you did not need much money to get enough to eat. There was none of the grinding poverty that existed in much of the East, including Hong Kong, and I do not recall ever seeing a beggar in Bangkok.

The klongs, which were not a bit like the canals of Venice, have since been filled in, but in those days they were a breeding ground for mosquitoes. When I say that the mosquitoes were as big as dragonflies, I exaggerate, but not much. Before we went, Deirdre was told that in the evenings all the ladies wore skirts down to their ankles to keep the mosquitoes from biting them, so she got such a skirt made but never wore it, as mosquito netting on doors and windows had come into fashion by the time we got there.

There were other, smaller insects which came through the mosquito netting and used to cluster round the electric lights in the ceiling. They brought with them a selection of lizards which used to cling upside down round the lights to eat these insects. There was one pink type of lizard which was transparent so you could see a black lump of insects in its stomach. Mostly they just clung upside down on the ceiling but sometimes one would lose its footing and come down plop onto the table.

We lived in a little bungalow with two bedrooms, a living room and a bathroom. There was a separate kitchen at the back, which we rarely entered. The electricity supply was so weak that we could hardly see to read at night. We managed to get an air conditioner fitted in our bedroom, which was a help to sleep, but it only worked at about a quarter capacity owing to the feeble electricity. The bed was a sort of large wooden table with a thin hair mattress. I do not know why the beds in Bangkok never had springs or sprung mattresses, but they didn't. Sleeping on a thin hair mattress on a wooden table is a noisy business as if you turn over you are likely to hit the hard surface with your knee or elbow, and then it goes bang.

The bathroom was a rather good tiled room, of the sort which would now be called a wet room, but there was no hot water, nor, indeed was there a bath or shower. I suppose it was thought that in that very hot climate hot water was an unnecessary refinement, or else perhaps the electricity was not up to heating it. There was a basin at which you could wash, and a huge jar of tepid water out of which you ladled water over yourself, splashing it freely around the wet room.

You could not drink the water, and for this you had to buy the bottled sort. Normal people could wash in it, but across the road there was an American family with three children whom they used to shout at a lot, plus a baby which they used to wash in bottled water rather than risk the stuff out of the tap.

When we moved in, the staff establishment consisted of a cook-amah called Cookie, who had a shy daughter whom she kept in the background; a cheerful young man known as Kong Swan, meaning gardener who was indeed the gardener and was supposed to be the night watchman as well; and a pye dog called Pom Pom.

In the street outside, as in most streets, was a pack of stray dogs, many of which were mangy and any one of which might be rabid. There was an explanation for the stray dogs. The Thais, being Buddhists, do not like killing things, and furthermore were not very efficient at dealing with bitches in heat. If they found themselves with an unwanted litter of puppies, as often happened, they put them out on the street to fend for themselves, and if they survived, then of course they bred and multiplied. If the problem got too bad, Chinese dog catchers were hired to round them up and put them down, which reduced the number but never got rid of them altogether. We never came across a mad dog, but we knew someone who had been bitten by one, and we thought that if Pom Pom was going to keep company with any of the street dogs she had better be vaccinated, so we took her to the vet. This was mostly for our sake, as we did not want her to go mad and bite us, but also for hers, as she was a friendly little dog to whom we warmed as we got to know her.

As if to prove that it was unwise to drink the water, and possibly wise to bath babies in bottled water, there was an outbreak of cholera soon after we got there, in which a thousand people died. So, having got Pom Pom vaccinated against rabies we got Cookie, her daughter, Kong Swan and ourselves inoculated against cholera. The doctor did not just give us an anti cholera jab, but one which dealt with typhoid and something called TAB as well. The effect was terrible and we all felt awful.

That night, as I lay on our hard, uncomfortable table-top bed in our extremely hot bedroom, suffering from a sore arm and a high temperature, there was a banging and shouting from the garden outside. Obviously this was something for Kong Swan to deal with in his role of night watchman, but, as I learnt later, he was cowering in the back of the car, in a state of misery at the cholera jab and terror at the man who was making the noise. In desperation I went out in my pyjamas and came up against a wild young man who was making a lot of noise and who shouted at me in Siamese. I shouted at him in English and pointed meaningfully at the garden gate. He shouted some more, I shouted back, and then he went out slamming the gate behind him, and I went back to bed.

The next morning our landlady, who lived next door, came round to explain and apologise. The young man was someone whom she had adopted. Occasionally when the moon was full he had some sort of a fit and behaved in a strange way, but he was, she assured us, entirely harmless. In this, I am sorry to say, she was wrong. About a year later when I suppose the moon was once more full, he had another of these fits and turned upon our landlady. She locked herself in her room, but he got a drill, drilled round the lock and stabbed her to death. She, poor terrified lady, was shouting for me to come to her rescue, but it all happened on one of the rare weekends when we had gone away to the seaside, so I was not there to hear. Cookie told us all about it when we got back. She and Kong Swan had heard it happening and I suppose if I had been present I would have hurried round and either saved our landlady or got stabbed myself.

The young Thai couple who lived on the other side were a lot more peaceful. She was called Nit and he was called Pracharn, and they behaved exactly as friendly people would behave in England. They came round to say hello, they invited us in for drinks, and we became friends. They came with us more than once to the seaside and possibly were with us when our landlady was killed. There was no kind of foreign enclave in Bangkok. The Americans with the baby moved away soon after we arrived, and we were then the only foreigners in our street, but it did not feel any different from living among neighbours at home.

This prompts me to make some observations about the Thai people in general. Being very clever, they managed to avoid being annexed into the British Empire, along with Burma and Malaya, or absorbed into French Indo-China along with Vietnam, Laos and Cambodia. Having always been independent in fact, the whole nation seemed to remain independent in spirit. They leaned towards the British in several ways – the foreign language in general use was English, not French; a lot of their many princes were educated in England, there were a number of long-established British companies in Thailand – but as they had never been a colony there was no feeling of colonial resentment.

Deirdre and I lived the most cosmopolitan multi-national existence that it is possible to imagine, she because she got a job with the South East Asia Treaty Organisation, and I because the airline business is necessarily a mixture of nationalities.

What, you may ask, is or was the South East Asia Treaty Organisation? It was like NATO only it was Seato, if you see what I mean, with its headquarters in Bangkok. They started it in 1955, the year after the Vietnamese had beaten the French, and they closed it down in 1977, four years after they had beaten the Americans. It was officially described as a regional defence organisation. The members were Australia, France, New Zealand, Pakistan, the Philippines, Thailand, the UK and the USA. They had lovely air-conditioned offices, which is what drew Deirdre to apply to them for a job, and all the perks which people in international organisations give themselves, such as big tax-free salaries plus duty-free drink and motor cars. I don't quite know what they did in their offices, but I believe they drew up plans, wrote reports and from time to time they held conferences in one or other of the member countries.

You might think that Seato would have played some part in the Vietnam war, but I have read two histories of that war and looked through another, and as far as I can see, it didn't. Australia and New Zealand were involved, but independently and not as part of a Seato force. In 1958, when we arrived, things in Vietnam were comparatively quiet; compared, that is, to what was to follow in what U Thant, Secretary General of the United Nations, described as "one of the most barbarous wars in history". The creeping involvement of American military advisers must have started, but not a lot was known generally. I expect that Deirdre could have told me exactly what they all did, but she wouldn't have done so because she was something to do with security, and security people of her generation never told you anything.

She got her job by a stroke of good luck. She went along in the hope that they might have an air-conditioned vacancy and it turned out that the Head of Security was someone seconded from her own London office who wanted an assistant, and he took her on at once. She did not get a princely salary or lavish perks but she got a great many friends such as a sweet Filipina girl called Cora, two glorious Thai girls called Bang Orn and Boon Krong, and the daughter of the Pakistani ambassador called Pam. She liked her boss and his wife, and there were some interesting people, including a strange hypochondriac Frenchman who was always ready to discuss his symptoms, and a very tall man called Police Major Prasart Panyarachun.

One of Deirdre's duties, as part of the security arrangements, was to hold a key to the office. So one evening, a big duty-free car drew up outside our house and out got Police Major Prasart Panyarachun in his grey police uniform with a pistol strapped to his side. I was sitting on the balcony in a rocking chair.

"Hello Prasart," I said, for we had met several times so I knew him quite well. "Come in."

"Is Mrs Enfield at home?"

"No, Prasart. She has gone to church, but she will be back soon. Come in and have a drink."

So I settled him in a chair with a whisky and soda and he explained the reason for his visit. He was to fly to New Zealand to a conference in two days' time but had left his ticket and his cash and his travellers cheques in his office desk and he was afraid they might be stolen. Did I think Mrs Enfield would mind going back to the office to let him retrieve them?

"Well Prasart, since you ask me, she probably will mind, but she will certainly do it for you. She has done a day's work and been to church and she will think she can now relax so she may be a bit cross, but don't worry – I promise you she will do it."

So we chatted for a time, and then he said "Do you think Mrs Enfield will really mind?"

"Prasart don't worry. She will probably be a little annoyed, but I absolutely guarantee that she will do it for you. Have another drink."

So we talked some more until he said "You really think Mrs Enfield will mind?"

"Prasart, you asked me, and I cannot help saying that I think, when she gets back, she may be a bit cross at having to go out again, but it is quite all right - she will certainly do it."

At this Police Major Prasart Panyarachun, although fortified with two whiskies, standing 6ft 2inches in his grey police uniform and with his pistol strapped to his side, rose to his feet.

"I think I will leave it," he said. Then he got in his car and drove off, to make his escape before Deirdre, who stands 5ft 3ins, could come back and say, "Oh Prasart how could you be so silly!"

My contribution to our joint multi-national acquaintance came from the other airlines. I suppose that the people in the various embassies all knew each other, and so did we in the airline business. Our offices were close together, in or near Suriwongse Road, which at that time could have been regarded as the main street of Bangkok, though I once was held up by a herd of goats being driven down the middle of it. The Cathay Pacific office was in the Trocadero Hotel, as was that of BOAC, and the bar of the Troc was a regular lunchtime meeting place for airline managers who could be French, English, Indian, Australian, Japanese, Dutch or American.

Our closest friend from among the airlines was Malcolm Barretto of Air India. The name is obviously Portuguese, and I got the impression that Air India was run by people with Portuguese names as Malcolm's confederates in other places seemed to be called da Silva, Pinto or Guterriez. I fear that Malcolm, good fellow though he was, had mildly racist tendencies. He had an Indian subordinate whom he addressed abruptly as "Kapoor" rather in the manner of a District Commissioner addressing the punkah wallah. Kapoor was obliged to call him Mr Barretto, whereas it was Malcolm and DC between him and the ground engineer DC Fernandez. Malcolm had a nice wife called Phyllis; Kapoor was single; DC was a rake, and we got to know them all because of Mr Bhattacharjee.

One day, as I sat in my room I heard a great noise coming from the outer office. When I went to investigate I found an Indian man at the counter trying to buy tickets, two small Indian children screaming and an imposing Indian lady in a beautiful sari who was absolutely, classically mad. She might almost have been auditioning for the part of Ophelia in Hamlet, singing little bits of song, repeating snatches of nursery rhymes, lapsing into Hindi or whatever was her native language, and all the time dancing up and down and waving her arms. Plate glass windows do not bulge, but our office window would have bulged if it could, from the pressure of tri-shaw coolies, street food vendors and other locals all pressing their noses against it as they gazed in at this extraordinary spectacle.

My first step was to move the Indian party into my office, where the children screamed a little more quietly, the mother continued to dance in the corner, and Mr Bhattacharjee, for that was his name, told me that they had come from Penang that day by train and now they wanted to fly to Calcutta. His wife had been perfectly normal when they set off but had got into this alarming state when they reached Bangkok. I explained to Mr Bhattacharjee that with his wife in this condition they could not possibly travel on one of our planes.

"What am I to do?" he said.

That was a good question. "I think we had better get your wife to a doctor."

Supposing that an Indian doctor would be best, I rang Malcolm Barretto who gave me the name and address of a doctor Joseph. I got my car, parked it outside the office, asked the girls to look after the children and ushered Mr and Mrs Bhattacharjee into the street, at which point Mrs Bhattacharjee ran away. That is, she ran off down Suriwongse Road for about 100 yards, shouting and singing on the way. With great difficulty we persuaded her to come back and get in my car, and with a lot more difficulty we got her into Dr Joseph's surgery. "I will send her to a hospital," he said. "Leave her to me." So we did, and as we drove away there was a sound of breaking glass and smashing furniture. Dr Joseph asked me plaintively afterwards why I brought her to him, and I gathered that she had done a lot of damage to his surgery when he tried to give her a sedative injection.

Mr Bhattacharjee decided to go back to Penang. He gave me his address, I drove him and his children to the station, he got on the train and disappeared, abandoning his wife into my care.

Dr Joseph told me that he had sent Mrs Bhattacharjee to the Bangkok Mental Hospital, and Deirdre and I worried about her. We had no idea what the Bangkok Mental Hospital was like. For all we knew it might be a sort of Victorian Bedlam with patients housed on straw and chained to the wall. Whatever it was like, to be shut up in a mental hospital in a foreign country where you didn't speak the language must be a frightening thing and to come to your senses and find that this had happened might be positively terrifying. We thought we had better go to see her.

If ever I need to be put in a mental hospital, I should like to go to the Bangkok one, if only it wasn't so far away. It proved to be very spacious, set in extensive grounds and there were lots of trim little Thai nurses in white uniforms who treated Mrs Bhattacharjee as if she were an honoured guest. She received us (there is no other word for it, as she was a most dignified person) in a little thatched summerhouse in the garden. She was perfectly calm, but the conversation got nowhere, as all she could say in English was "my baby, my baby" at the same time making baby-rocking motions with her hands, so we supposed that there was a baby in Penang which she was missing.

We went away feeling reassured. Two of the girls in the office took an interest and went to visit her, but Dr Joseph told us to stop it as she was best left undisturbed.

After three weeks or so Dr Joseph told me she was fit to travel, so I sent a telegram to Mr Bhattacharjee and in due course he arrived by train from Penang. I met him at the station and we went to the hospital. After a short pause Mrs Bhattacharjee came to meet us in a manner worthy of the Maharani of Baroda or some similar female potentate. She did not walk, she stalked, advancing in a stately manner resplendent in her beautiful sari, with a little Thai nurse trotting along behind her holding a parasol over her head. The meeting of wife and husband, as I recall, was entirely unemotional. They got quietly into the car, we went back to the station and off they went to Penang. Mr Bhattacharjee later sent me a letter and a Parker pen, which was nice of him. In his letter he said that he was grateful to have found so many kind people in Bangkok, and the curious thing is that I have no recollection of any money changing hands. I myself certainly did not part with any, I do not think the hospital presented Mr Bhattacharjee with a bill, and I do not think Dr Joseph was in any way recompensed for the damage done to his surgery, all of which was kind, I agree.

And what, you may ask, has any of this to do with Malcolm Barretto? I rather hesitate to explain, but there were a few days between the time that Dr Joseph said Mrs Bhattacharjee was fit to travel and the day when Mr Bhattacharjee could come to collect her. Thinking that, nice as the mental hospital was, she might rather be out of it than in it, I said that we had a spare room and perhaps she could spend this interval with us. Dr Joseph vetoed the idea out of hand, and I can see it was a daft suggestion but it seemed reasonable at the time. Anyway, Dr Joseph told Malcolm and Malcolm's reaction, as he told me later, was to wonder who was the young Englishman who had arrived from nowhere and invited strange Indian women into his house? His curiosity being aroused, he went out

130

of his way to get to know us, and before long we had reached the stage that a car would often draw up outside our house and honk its horn, then Malcolm would shout, "Come on Ed and Deirdre – we're going to the cinema" and off we would go along with Phyllis and Kapoor and sometimes DC Fernandez.

I may say that cinemas in Bangkok were properly conducted, much as they used to be in England before the rot set in. At the end of each performance a picture of the king appeared on the screen and we all stood to attention while the national anthem was played. The Thai national anthem is extremely long, so we stood for about the equivalent of three verses of God Save the Queen. As it drew to a close we all with one accord bowed deeply from the waist towards the king's picture. No one would have dreamt of leaving before the last note of the national anthem, which was a sign of the enormous popularity of King Bhumibol Adulyadej who, as I write this, is the world's longest reigning monarch. I have always had the greatest admiration for King Bhumibol since I saw him, on a newsreel, conducting an audience with the Prime Minister and the Leader of the Opposition. The rule as propounded in The King and I is that the head must not be higher than king's, and as King Bhumibol was sitting on a chair, the politicians were obliged to sit on the floor. They settled themselves at a respectful distance but he signalled to them to come closer, so they had to slither towards him across the carpet. After this, as I understood it, he gave them some kind of reproof or even, perhaps, tore them off a strip. What a wonderful thing it would be, I thought, if this was the way of things in England. If only Her Majesty the Queen could send for the Prime Minister and the Leader of the Opposition and tell them, while they sat on the floor, that it was time they stopped their childish brawling in the House of Commons and restored some dignity to the offices which they held.

Our social life, as well as trips to the cinema, took in quite a lot of dancing as many of the restaurants had dance bands and dance floors. Malcolm had rather a good singing voice and liked to get hold of the microphone and sing if he could. He had a particularly awful version of Love is a Many-Splendored Thing as part of his repertoire. Rather than listening to Malcolm Barretto singing we liked watching Madeleine Vlachos and Ma Chan Ling dancing the cha cha. Madeleine was something of a mystery. She was Greek by nationality but spoke no word of Greek and had never been to Greece. By birth she was half Greek and half Chinese, and this was a very successful combination as she was gloriously attractive. She was petite, young, had a Grecian profile, and as well as Chinese spoke perfect English as if she was an American. She worked for Northwest Airlines, though what she did or why they had an office was itself a bit of a mystery, as they had no flights to Bangkok, just an office consisting of Madeleine and an American called Ron. The greater mystery, though, was how she came to be in Bangkok anyway. She never mentioned any parents, she had no visible boyfriend, she never explained where she came from or where else she had been. It was rumoured that she had a broken heart, but if so, it did not show. There was about her a certain reserve which stopped us from asking questions and almost the only thing we knew was that she had a rich cousin, a prosperous Chinese businessman called Ma Chan Ling, with whom she danced the cha cha.

His name, as he explained to us, meant Handsome Horse God. Handsome Horse God was very tall and Madeleine was, as I have said, petite. The cha cha was much in vogue, and when they danced it together he danced with great energy and bold steps, and she demurely with tiny steps. The combined effect was so brilliant that they became famous for it, and once they took the floor all other couples would drift back to their seats to watch, and clap like anything when the music finally stopped.

We saw a lot of Madeleine and Chan Ling, to give him his proper name. He had a couple of horses somewhere, one of which I rode, and he had a boat behind which we all went water-skiing. In his spare time I think he may have dabbled in espionage as he was very friendly with a man at the British Embassy who was certainly a spy.

I will not give his real name, as spies do not like to be exposed even if they must have been retired for years and are quite possibly dead. His first name, however, was Michael, and as pronounced by Chan Ling in his Chinese intonation, the name in full sounded like My Kul Click Click. He had the sort of official title that such people have, calling himself Trade Secretary or something like that, but I know that Click Click was a spy because Deirdre could tell at once. Those in the espionage business have a sort of freemasonry among themselves, and while they may not go in for secret handshakes or anything like that, one of them can always spot another straight away. Not being sure whether he was MI6 or MI5 Deirdre asked him the sort of coded question that those on the inside do ask of each other, along the lines of "Are you A branch or Q branch?" or possibly "Are you A2 or A4?" and he got frightfully cross as he said she might have blown his cover. Anyway, from the answer she concluded that he was MI6, a spy, and not MI5, a counter spy.

Goodness knows who he spied on or what business of the British it was, whoever his targets may have been or whatever they got up to. The Chinese Embassy in Bangkok represented the rump of the Kuo Min Tang in Taiwan, and not the communist mainland, so there was no point in infiltrating that. Although I never met a Russian anywhere I suppose there might have been a Russian Embassy in Bangkok, and perhaps Click Click had it bugged. If he was any good as a spy he may have given the ambassador advance notice of the little revolution that took place one day, though there was nothing to be done about it and it didn't seem to matter very much.

It was perhaps more of a coup than a revolution. As we went to our different offices one morning we found the streets lined with soldiers and tanks. The next morning they had gone away, and we read in the newspaper that the prime minister had been replaced by a field marshal. After that everything seemed to go on as normal until Chinese New Year. It was, I was told, the custom among Chinese merchants that they should settle their debts at the New Year, and it was such a loss of face for those who could not come up with the money that it was common practice for the defaulter to set his house on fire and pay his debts with the insurance money. This year the house of some unfortunate Chinese businessman went up in flames as the New Year approached and the field marshall had him shot out of hand, after which no more Chinese houses caught fire. This was the only dictatorial episode that we were aware of and in other ways the military regime, which I think was temporary, did not seem to be oppressive and the change was generally thought to be an improvement over what had gone before.

Life in the office went on smoothly enough, but with a bit of added interest when I singlehandedly uncovered a smuggling ring, and an unfortunate episode when I found the trusted chief clerk had been stealing our money.

The episode of the smuggling ring sounds as if I had embarked on a dangerous undertaking like one of Enid Blyton's Famous Five, but I managed it without ever moving from my office desk. There was a rule that we might carry company mail on our planes, but nothing that was not strictly a matter of our own business, or we would infringe the monopoly of the Thai post office. One day the Customs came on board, opened the mailbag, found some private correspondence and fined us. After this a decree went forth that we were to be extra careful and I ruled that the incoming mailbag, which the chief clerk used to open, should in future be brought to me. One day I found a handwritten letter in Chinese writing which, whatever it was, can have had nothing to do with official business, so I sent it back to Hong Kong. It was, they told me, to do with the smuggling of rubies. The plan to be followed, according to the letter, was that real rubies should be declared and shipped as artificial rubies, with some artificial ones scattered on the top of the container. You might not think this a very exciting form of smuggling, as smuggling goes, but unfortunately the mastermind of the operation was an extremely capable Chinese woman who was absolutely the key figure in the Hong Kong passenger department, and they felt obliged to give her the sack. This was very hard on her boss, who had been used to presiding over the department in a benevolent way but leaving all the real work to her. Curiously, I never heard who the letter was intended for in Bangkok, and as I had no wish to sack anybody, I took good care not to enquire.

The matter of the chief clerk was altogether more distressing. He had been left in control of the ticket stock, and I can only assume that my predecessor never carried out a check because the amount stolen came to about £3,000 which, in today's money would amount to a tidy sum, at least £100,000 if not more. He managed to help himself to our cash by the simple but easily detectable device of selling tickets from the bottom of the pile and pocketing the money. The tickets all had serial numbers, and when the missing ones came up to be accounted for, he simply sold some more off the bottom of the next pile, and so it went on. After I had been there for a few weeks I got round to checking the tickets and it all came out. He confessed without difficulty and told me that he'd taken the money to pay gambling debts and so it was all gone.

He had to go the way of the lady in the Hong Kong passenger department, but the question arose as to whether he should be handed over to the police. The people in Hong Kong said he should, and I said he shouldn't. Very likely I was wrong. They took the simple view that if you steal your employer's money you are likely to be put in jail. That is the way it is, everybody knows this, so you have no right to complain if it happens. I did not want him to go to jail partly because I quite liked the chap, partly because he had a wife and two very sweet children (most Thai children are sweet) and partly perhaps because I was green and inexperienced and did not appreciate the full weight of my employer's argument.

My main reason, though, was something different, and here I must be careful or I will bring myself within the scope of the Race Relations Act. The general view at that time was that if you were running a business in Bangkok you should proceed on the basis that if you gave anyone a chance to steal your money they would certainly take it. When I told the head of the Borneo Company that I had found the chief clerk had been stealing our cash, he, a wise man with a lifetime's experience, threw up his hands in mock horror and said, "In Bangkok? Impossible!" Such things could happen at any level. While we were there they put the finance minister in prison for embezzling public funds and I do not think it occasioned any great surprise.

I suppose, in brief, that my view was similar to the rule in the days when people had servants, that you should not put temptation in their way by leaving money lying around. Anyway, I sent a plea to Hong Kong saying that in view, as it were, of the custom of the country, he had been unfairly tempted and please would they let him off. They allowed me to have my way and in due course he got a job with another airline, so perhaps from his point of view it was a most satisfactory episode. Whether it will count for or against me on the Day of Judgement is something I shall be interested to learn.

I have said there was quite a lot of dancing going on, and I did some dancing in the way of business. I am not much of a dancer. Ma Chan Ling tried to teach me the cha cha, clumping to and fro in his riding boots across the floor of our sitting room, but I never really got the hang of it. In spite of my general incompetence and dislike of the pastime, from time to time I used to go dancing in the company of Kingsweet Y.T. Chen, the Chinese sales manager.

There were many nightclubs in Bangkok where there were taxi dancers. The girls were either Thai or Chinese and you paid them for their company by the hour. The Thai girls were generally prettier and their hourly rate was lower, but Chinese businessmen liked to dance with Chinese girls, who had to be imported from Hong Kong and therefore cost more per hour to dance with. Fortunately for Cathay Pacific the Thai government would only give dancing girls visas for three months at a time, so they had to keep flying back to Hong Kong to get new visas, after which they flew back to Bangkok. Somehow YT Chen had completely cornered the market in dancing girls, and they all flew Cathay Pacific. He thought it important that we should keep in touch with this valuable trade and so from time to time I would explain to Deirdre that I had to work late, then YT and I would go on a round of the nightclubs. I would much rather have danced with the Thai girls if I had to dance at all, but business is business, so I shuffled around the floor with a Chinese dancing girl, chatted for a time with the nightclub owner, paid up and went on with YT to the next club. The company allowed us a small amount for entertaining, which I split between YT and me, and we spent it all on dancing girls. I may say that it is the only aspect of the airline business in which I did not encounter any opposition, as we never ran into any other airline managers on a similar mission.

*

Of all the many friendships we made in Bangkok the best and longest lasting was with Bunny and Maureen Broome. Their name was not really Broome but Chakrabandhu, and his name was not Bunny but Bongsebrahma, and he was a superior member of the royal family with the title of Mom Rajawongse. As a young man he spent time in England and to call him Mom Rajawongse Bongsebrahma Chakrabandhu was altogether too much for one of his English landladies, who mangled it into Bunny Broome, which stuck. He was a man of many talents. When we met, he was running a successful interior design business called Broome Studios, but he had been educated originally as a soldier, both in Thailand and in England. He was sent to school at Hailebury, was commissioned from Sandhurst into the East Yorkshire Regiment, and later rose to the rank of lieutenant colonel in the Thai army. By far his greatest public service was to run the wartime prison camp in which most of the foreigners in Thailand were interned, including many of his friends.

Bunny was born in 1906, so at the time of Pearl Harbour in December 1941 he was probably 36 years old. The Thais, being very clever, waited to see who was going to win the war, and when a Japanese victory seemed certain they quickly declared war on their side and against us. Their first act was to round up all the British and put them into an internment camp, with Bunny in charge.

I knew several people who had been locked up under his command, and they spoke of him with the greatest possible gratitude. One of them told me that on Sundays Bunny used to let the prisoners out under guard to visit non-combatants, such as the Swiss or Swedes, or the French, whose Vichy government was on the Japanese side. The prisoner would have lunch with the family and the guard with the servants in the kitchen. On one occasion the prisoner went to collect his guard but found him asleep, so he went back to camp without him. To the delight of the inmates, Bunny then put up a notice which read:

All prisoners returning from leave
will ensure
that they bring their guards with them.

Bunny and Maureen were both killed in a car crash in 1971, and their family published a memorial booklet which includes a letter signed by eight ex internees, part of which reads as follows:

"Those of us whose signatures appear below, as well as many other Civilians interned in Thailand during the 1941/45 War in the Far East, and several former residents of Bangkok, who would we know like their names to be coupled with ours, are writing to express our deep sorrow on hearing, earlier this month, about the tragic death of our old friend, Mom Rajawongse Bongsephrom Chakrabandhu and his Wife, Maureen.

Although over 25 years have elapsed since the end of the War, the passing of time has done nothing to dim our recollection of how much we owe to Mom Bongsephrom for his work as Camp Commandant. The fact that some of us are alive and in good health is in no small measure due to the efforts he made to ensure the provision of a very reasonable standard of comfort and of medical facilities for us during the four years of internment, when supplies of so many of the necessities of Life were difficult to obtain."

The photographs in the book include one of Bunny in the centre of a group of happy, smiling people with the caption, *"Taken after the relief of the Internees"* and another of Bunny with five healthy, cheerful-looking fellows, one with a pipe in his mouth, and the caption *"With members of the Committee of Internees."*

That he was able to run the camp as he did was due to his personal courage. I do not believe that this was generally known, but I discovered it one night when he and Maureen were staying with us in England. Our wives had gone to bed, we were sipping our drinks by the fire and he told me that one day, the guard commander burst into his office, shouting, "Mom, come quickly! Japanese soldiers!"

At the gate he found a group of Japanese climbing out of their lorry and wanting to come into the camp and beat up some prisoners.

"I had prepared for this," said Bunny "I had drilled the guard in what to do, so I gave the order 'Form up, the guard!' and they formed up across the gateway.

'Now go away' I said, but the Japanese took no notice and kept on coming. Then I drew my sword, and at this the guard brought their loaded rifles up into the aim.

'Go away,' I said but the Japanese came right up to the gateway. Then I raised my sword, and there was a *click*, as the guard released the safety catches of their rifles.

'When I drop my sword the guard will fire, so go away!'

At this they turned round and got back in their lorry and left. A little while later a Japanese officer arrived. 'You would like to see the camp? Certainly! Some of your men were here a little while ago, rather out of hand but it is all dealt with. Let me show you round.' So I showed him round," said Bunny. "After that I didn't have any trouble".

I asked the obvious question: "Would you really have dropped your sword and shot some of the Japanese?"

"Of course. If I hadn't I would have had no authority afterwards."

I have said that this was our longest-lasting Bangkok friendship, and it has extended through three generations. Maureen was not Thai but was half Malay, half Irish and a Catholic, and as our eldest daughter was conceived in Bangkok, Maureen became one of her godmothers. She and Bunny did not exactly keep in touch, but after we came home they used to arrive unannounced at irregular intervals, and come to see us. They came once with their sons Paddy and Sandy, and required us to place them both in a Catholic public school without delay. The best we could do at short notice was to get them into a new school called Redrice. I knew almost nothing about it so I was a bit worried, especially when it went out of business quite quickly, but it lasted long enough for Paddy and Sandy, and Paddy always spoke well of Redrice and was upset when he found that it had closed. Then, years later, Paddy himself made a similar sudden descent upon us, this time with his wife Sue and bringing his daughter Pinkie and his son Paul. These two we were required, as before, to get into suitable schools almost at once. Pinkie we consigned to Roedean, and Paul to Charterhouse, and from each establishment they were triumphantly expelled. In neither case was it for any exciting or disgraceful act, but simply because of an incurable habit of disappearing to London to live it up with other Thai students of their acquaintance. It was all a great success. Paddy and Sandy are both prosperous businessmen; Pinkie is lovely, happily married and has a thriving business of her own; Paul came to see us not long ago on a mission to invest in property in London, his pockets bulging with other people's money.

Envoi

After five exciting years in the Far East, including fourteen glorious months in Bangkok doing the best job I ever had in my life, we decided to come home. There were a number of reasons, the main one being that we did not like the idea of leaving in England any children we might have, while we were shuttled about between Hong Kong, Japan, Bangkok or Australia, which was what we could have been faced with had we stayed.

It was the custom when people left Bangkok for all their friends to come to the airport to see them off, and we have a great many photographs of the occasion. There they all are, Bunny and Maureen, Bang Orn and Boon Krong, Tweetie, Y.T. Chen, Malcolm Barretto and DC Fernandez, the Third Secretary of the Embassy, and others who have got into this book and yet others who have not, and with Deirdre weeping behind her sunglasses.

Christopher Ryder, who came to replace me, was with us the night before when the office staff gave us a dinner at which Kingsweet YT Chen made the following speech:

Ladies & Gentlemen,

Tonight we are here having a party for farewell to Mr. & Mrs. Enfield and also to welcome Mr. Ryder. We are really feeling a satisfaction and happy time at the moment.

Mr. & Mrs. Enfield came here on May of last year. Mr. Enfield has done such a lot of work for C.P.A., and Mrs. Enfield also has given a lot of help. Of course we have seen from the result and the sales figure is straight up, and led the staff gone to the right way in fourteen months during is staying in Bangkok.

Now, Mr. Enfield for his own future, wants to return to his mother country – England – so we are feeling sad for our Virtuous and talent leader leaving from us so soon, but we hope they may come to see us again after they have successfully settled down at home.

Well, we are also feeling happy to welcome the Virtuous and wise new manager Mr. Ryder, Mr. Ryder has been educated in the same university as Mr. Enfield, and worked at the Butterfield and Swire Co. Ltd., already two and a half years. He has proved his ability in Japan and Hong Kong. Mr. Ryder will take us to continue and carry on business side, as well as he can, I am quite sure that C.P.A.'s business will progress like the Sun at Sunrise.

Well, ladies and gentlemen, let us drink to their health and wishing Mr. & Mrs. Enfield have a nice trip and arriving home safely and may God Bless Them.

Thank you!

They gave us a silver salver engraved with all their names, and to say we were touched would be to understate it greatly. I almost felt the need for sunglasses on my own account.

We set off for home by an unusual route, as if we were determined to test the theory that the earth is round, and to see if we could get back to where we started by keeping going East. We flew from Bangkok to Tokyo and from Tokyo to Vancouver, and there we got on the famous Canadian Pacific train which crosses Canada in three days. We thought this would be a rest because you would think that sitting on a train with nothing to do but eat, read and look out of the window would be restful, but it turned out to be exhausting.

It was the strain of doing nothing that was the tiring bit. On the first day the train passes through the Rocky Mountains, and as we were never likely to see the Rocky Mountains again we felt obliged to sit in the glass-domed observation car and look at them. They are very magnificent, but the truth is that one Rocky Mountain looks much like another, so after you have been looking out for an hour or two, gently swaying in your seat while the train rattles over the rails making a noise like "gruddley-pod, gruddley-pod," there seems to be a certain sameness to the proceedings. You can go to your bedroom and read, occasionally glancing out of the window to make sure the Rockies are still there, and the day is punctuated by meals at which you tend to over-eat as there is not much else to do. On the second day the train goes through the prairies, and, as with the Rockies, one bit of prairie is much like another - then on the third day the view is largely of Christmas trees, and as each tree is much the same as the last there is not a lot to break the monotony. What you want to do, but cannot, is to take some exercise. The train does stop occasionally, but we never dared to get off for more than a couple of minutes in case it blew its whistle and roared off, leaving us on the platform at somewhere like Moose Jaw, Saskatchewan - or possibly Medicine Hat. (I am not certain that the train took in Moose Jaw and Medicine Hat, but I hope it did, as I like to think I have been to places with such excellent names, even if I was only passing through.)

Travelling like this seemed to bring on a sort of lethargic torpor, in which state we stumbled off the train at Toronto, into the arms of my Aunt Helen and the friendly grasp of my Uncle Morris. There had been an irregular flow of letters between us since I last saw them, when I was fourteen, and it was the greatest pleasure to see them again after a lapse of fifteen years. They had moved from Ottawa to a place called Beamsville, by Lake Ontario, where Uncle Morris was partly a fruit farmer and partly a businessman. In his role as a fruit farmer he had a cherry orchard with pie-plates hung on all the trees. The Canadians were ahead of us in the matter of fast food; they no longer baked pies but bought them ready-made, on tin plates which Uncle Morris hung on the trees to scare off the birds. As a businessman he used to go off to an office several times a week, and, the weather being fine, on his return he always, as ever, enquired of the dog: "Are you a hot dog?"

Aunt Helen was as kind and welcoming as ever. I got on better with Ron than I had before. Their niece Peggy, from Kirk's Ferry days, came to see us with a husband and baby, but her sister Caroline could not. This was a pity as I would have liked to ask after her beautiful friend Natalie with whom I had been so desperately in love, and who would have let me be her feller if only I had been two years older. After five days we flew to England, where things came, as it were, full circle. I got a job, and we bought a cottage, in Sussex. It was about two miles from my parents' former home where Randolph Churchill got stuck in the mud so I was, in truth, back where I started.

It was a time when package holidays were just getting going, and people with whom I worked used to fly off for fortnights in places we had never heard of, such as Alicante, or places with unlikely names, such as the Costa Brava. We could not afford to do such things, but we did not mind. Deirdre had been in Egypt before she went to Hong Kong, and what was Alicante to Egypt and Thailand? What was a Spanish package holiday when set against Japan and Bangkok? We, who had circled the globe, could afford to stay smugly at home, with children whom we took once a year to Devon or the New Forest. Otherwise we remained, like Randolph Churchill, in the Sussex mud which, as I write, is where we still are.

Appendix

In writing about the classical syllabus of those days I have to rely on my memory, which is not always a sound source of information. In this case, though, I think that if someone were to dig out of the archives a copy of the Examination Statutes for 1948 they would find that what follows is pretty accurate, at least in respect of Mods.

For Honour Moderations we were required to read and be ready to translate from:

1) The whole of the *Iliad* and *Odyssey*.

2) The complete works of Virgil.

3) Five Latin books - a play of Plautus, for example, or a speech of Cicero counting as one book.

4) Five Greek books, similar to 3

For 5) we had to translate from English into Latin prose, and for 6) into Greek prose. They set quite difficult proses. I remember the words, "We step forward with such hopes as religion or philosophy afford" from Gibbon, I think, as part of the passage to be turned into Latin.

7) and 8) were pieces of Greek and Latin prose and verse, to be translated unseen into English.

9) and 10) were the two papers which needed the most preparation. There were three Latin and three Greek books from which you had to be prepared both to translate and also to comment on the grammatical and literary niceties. Also, in one of the three you had to be ready to discuss the different manuscript readings. The Latin books in my case were the first three books of the De Rerum Natura of Lucretius, and the first two words of the third book are, in different manuscripts, either *O tenebris*, *E tenebris* or *A tenebris*. If these appeared in the examination paper, you were expected to weigh up the merits of O, E, and A and plump for one of them in a judicious manner. This is an easy example, but there is one line where the manuscripts read, "*Magnis concede necesse est*", which means "Make way for large men - you must." This makes no sense in the context, but I have always thought it would be a good motto for the Univ boat club.

Paper 11) was a special subject, which in my case was the Greek Drama, and involved a close study of the Poetics of Aristotle (in Greek).

Paper 12) was a general paper in English, with such questions as "How would our estimation of Homer be altered if we had the *Iliad* but not the *Odyssey*, or the *Odyssey* but not the *Iliad*?" For those who have not read either, this is like saying "What difference would it make if we had Shakespeare's tragedies, but not the comedies?"

Then there were two optional papers in which you were given passages of English verse to render, in one case into Latin hexameters supposedly like those of Virgil, or elegiac couplets purportedly like those of Ovid, and in the other into Greek iambics intended to resemble those of Sophocles. I did these papers but I needn't have bothered as they did not do me any good.

The scoring system was quite ingenious. For a first, you had to get the equivalent of six alphas and no gammas. Two alpha/betas counted as one alpha, but a gamma cancelled an alpha. Thus you could get a first with, say, seven alphas, one gamma, and the rest betas, or, like me, with five alphas, two alpha/betas and no gamma. The verse papers counted if you did well, but not if you didn't, so in these you could get gammas and it did not matter, but if you got alphas, it helped.

All were three-hour papers except for Homer and Vergil, which took only one and a half hours. We wrote them at the rate of two a day, morning and afternoon, with a weekend break in the middle, and that in itself was a test of stamina. As I look back I am really quite surprised that I got through it all, but in this I was not exceptional as everyone managed somehow. There were a few short cuts, but not many. Someone had made a list of the more difficult passages of Homer, and if you mastered them, you could, if you liked, skip the rest of his works as some of these passages always turned up in the exam. Also, I had read a few of the required Latin and Greek books at school, so I did not read them again but trusted that I could remember them well enough when the time came. So, one way and another I scraped into a first.

My memory of Greats is not quite so sure. There were options available in ancient history, but not, I think, in philosophy. I know that we read Herodotus, Thucydides, *the Athenian Constitution of Aristotle*, *Selected Letters of Cicero* and the *Annals of Tacitus*. There was also a little green book called *Sources for Roman History BC 133-70*, which formed part of the syllabus, and when the time came bits from any of these could be served up in Greek or Latin for us to translate and comment on.

Turning to philosophy, as well as *the Republic* of Plato and Aristotle's *Ethics* we read briefly the classic philosophers like Locke, Descartes and Berkley, and joined in the game of Oxford chop-logic then fashionable among the followers of Wittgenstein and people like that. As well as all this we read learned articles in learned publications, and twice a week we read essays to our tutors, one in philosophy and one in ancient history. What really counted in Finals was the quality of our answers to the sort of wide-ranging questions they habitually set to students of history and philosophy.

I think I filled my Ancient History tutor George Cawkwell with increasing despair as time went on, as it became clear that I had obviously not got the hang of what I was supposed to do, and never produced anything faintly original or mildly interesting. The great philosopher Sir Peter Strawson, however, was kind enough to say that he thought I would go into the Examination Schools "very well equipped" but my friend George Byam-Shaw said this meant that my fountain pen would be full of ink and that I would not forget my handkerchief. I think he was right, as I ended up, as I have said, with an uninteresting second.

I suspect that the continual process of watering down has made things easier now, but in saying this I am well aware that much less was expected of us than of our fathers and grandfathers. Literary figures like Lord Byron or Sir Walter Scott, without any pretensions to being scholars, showed, in a casual way, far more knowledge of the classics than I ever attained, and by Dr Johnson's standards I emerged with a degree of ignorance of which a schoolboy would have been ashamed.

18047288R00081

Printed in Great Britain
by Amazon